MAPPING THE DELTA

George Szirtes was born in Budapest in 1948, and came to England with his family after the 1956 Hungarian Uprising. He was educated in England, training as a painter, and has always written in English. In recent years he has worked as a translator of Hungarian literature. He retired from teaching at the University of East Anglia in 2003, and lives in Wymondham, Norfolk.

His first collection, *The Slant Door*, was awarded the Geoffrey Faber Prize, and since then he has won the T.S. Eliot Prize and a Cholmondeley Award and been shortlisted for Whitbread and Forward Poetry Prizes. He was elected a Fellow of the Royal Society of Literature in 1982.

After his first return to Hungary in 1984 he translated poetry, fiction and plays from the Hungarian and for his work in this field he has won the European Poetry Translation Prize, the Dery Prize and been shortlisted for the Weidenfeld and Aristeion Prizes as well as receiving the Golden Star medal of the Hungarian republic. His translation of László Krasznahorkai's Satantango won the Best Translated Book Award in 2013, and was a Man Booker International winner in 2015, as translator of László Krasznahorkai.

With George Gömöri he co-edited Bloodaxe's *The Colonnade of Teeth: Modern Hungarian Poetry* (1996), and his Bloodaxe edition of Ágnes Nemes Nagy's poetry, *The Night of Akhenaton: Selected Poems* (2004), was a Poetry Book Society Recommended Translation. His study of the artist Ana Maria Pacheco, *Exercise of Power*, was published by Ashgate in 2001. He co-edited *An Island of Sound: Hungarian Poetry and Fiction before and beyond the Iron Curtain* (Harvill, 2004) and *In Their Own Words: Contemporary Poets on their Poetry* (Salt, 2012).

His Bloodaxe poetry titles include: *The Budapest File* (2000); *An English Apocalypse* (2001); *Reel* (2004), winner of the T.S. Eliot Prize; *New & Collected Poems* (2008); *The Burning of the Books and other poems* (2009); *Bad Machine* (2013); and *Mapping the Delta* (2016). *The Burning of the Books* and *Bad Machine* were both shortlisted for the T.S. Eliot Prize. *Bad Machine* and *Mapping the Delta* are both Poetry Book Society Choices. Bloodaxe has also published his Newcastle/Bloodaxe Poetry Lectures, *Fortinbras at the Fishhouses: Responsibility, the Iron Curtain and the sense of history as knowledge* (2010), and John Sears' critical study, *Reading George Szirtes* (2008).

GEORGE SZIRTES

Mapping the Delta

BLOODAXE BOOKS

ISBN: 978 1 78037 320 1

First published 2016 by
Bloodaxe Books Ltd
Eastburn
South Park
Hexham
Northumberland NE46 1BS

www.bloodaxebooks.com
For further information about Bloodaxe titles
please visit our website or write to
the above address for a catalogue.

Supported using public funding by

**ARTS COUNCIL
ENGLAND**

Printed in Great Britain by Bell & Bain Limited, Glasgow, Scotland, on
acid-free paper sourced from mills with FSC chain of custody certification.

For Clarissa, children and grandchildren

ACKNOWLEDGEMENTS

Acknowledgements are due to the editors of the following publications in which some of these poems first appeared: *The Ecchoing Green, ed. Richard Skinner* (The Big Blake Project, 2015), *Hwaet! 20 Years of Ledbury Poetry Festival*, ed. Mark Fisher (Bloodaxe Books, 2016), *Interlit Quarterly, Maghreb, Manhattan Review* (USA), *The Messenger, numero-cinq, Ploughshares* (USA), *The Poetry Mail* (India), *The Poetry Review, Prague Review, The Rotary Dial, The Stare's Nest, The Times Literary Supplement, The Rialto*, and *The Woven Tale*.

Some poems were published in an Eyewear Aviator pamphlet, *Notes on the Inner City* (2015). The sequence *The Mathematics of Freedom* was commissioned by Poet in the City and Archives for London for an event at Imperial College in December 2014, while 'The Drunken Boat' was commissioned by the Rimbaud and Verlaine Foundation. 'The Matrix Reloaded' was read by Patrick Stewart as part of a Voices for Choices literary event organised by Campaign for Dignity in Dying in May 2013.

CONTENTS

Mapping the Delta

For several months we had been moving down
the river when it broke into tight channels,
shores suddenly closer, a smear of green and brown
with a smattering of fishermen among runnels

silent then gone. It was disorientating
at first. We were drunk on the local wine
and unused to drifting around and waiting.
We were lost without landmark and sign.

And then a new channel opened and a craft
much like ours appeared and pushed ahead.
And then another. Everywhere fore and aft
there were boats and water that fed

still more water. We were everywhere
and nowhere at once in the humid air.

*

Who can define the river? Who can own
the stream as it moves, as it keeps breaking up
swollen by tributaries. Can anyone drown
in its confluent jargons or make the river stop

to admire itself? The cities it passes through
are habitations of only one kind. I've lived there
and walked embankments that were once new
but now are old. They were not an everywhere.

It was maps we needed to locate the voices
of the delta with its birdcalls and inflections,
the marshy ground that lay between places
that were solid with the chattering of fictions.

The boats were full of faces feeding the ocean.
The water moving, becoming the location.

*

Phalarope, egret, grebe, pelican, bittern
and heron, flamingo, spoonbill, ibis, names
of familiar fauna, the familiar pattern
of speech, the well-mapped language games...

We had endless supplies of thick black coffee
to keep us going. We spread out the maps
and named more fauna, strophe after strophe,
the delta was singing its versions of perhaps.

The river was charted but now the tide rises
and presses on and moves between tongues
of land to emerge in a mouth that blazes
with its own ideas, its own flickering songs.

There's no exhaustive language. The maps are a start
in gathering up strands of a notional heart.

In the Cinema Lobby

1

I was standing in the lobby of my mind
on the tiled floor beneath the colonnade,
the marble, the swags, the chandeliers, the bosses,
the whole baroque like a vast wedding cake
that's set to squash you, when the voices came.

They were the movies of a childhood game
where terror was the moment before the break,
where the present tense was pregnant with her losses
and scenes our fathers or our mothers made
that drove us deaf and left us mad and blind.

2

It was the glamorous era of first speaking,
of songs, and dancing feet, the costumes bright
as galaxies, the choreography of masters
with visions that prefigured the late war.
It was buoyant, fearsome, perfect, very loud,

and in my mind I was part of the great crowd
still jostling in the foyer or at the bar.
There were sylphs in satin draped round the pilasters
who'd remain there right through the long night,
who'd not mind gunfire or the roof leaking.

Central Europe

How admirable they are, these sober gentlemen
with their silver hair and patriotic moustaches,
their straight backs, their handsome, faintly malicious
smiles, their authority, their quiet gravamen.
They are assuredly the very soul of the nation,
who look to assure us and strive to look reassuring,
exemplars of uprightness, objects of admiration,
who have always been there and are the enduring
face of the people for which the nation has fought.
You couldn't imagine them with a gun by a ditch
surveying a row of corpses, perish the thought!
They wouldn't murder their despicable enemies,
they'd simply tidy them up like an unfortunate glitch
in the programme then straighten their sober grey ties.

Bartók

It wasn't a style as such, the way they wore
their hats and waistcoats, laboured through the mud
or gathered at the inn. Hard to make a score
of what they sang, the odd shriek and thud,
that nasal whine, the raw polyphony
of their existence. You had to record it all
on the latest equipment, pay them good money
for performing, listen to them call
the devil into the heart of the authentic,
his melancholy to the tongue's rough edge.
It can't have been easy to shift their strangely frantic
strings into the concert hall. It was knowledge
but not as we knew it, nor was it desired.
It screeched and snapped like bullets freshly fired.

Music was war. It was the sound of guns
wheeled into position and the cry of men
in ditches. Music was prophetic. Once
it lodged in the ear the worst would surely happen.
Those women were the wind howling. Rain
was rapid rifles. Concert halls were wrecked,
the century blown wide open. The troop train
would never arrive, and nothing would connect.
The barbarians were always at the gate,
but they were us and now we had burst in
to what we had forgotten. We were late:
our villages were bodies and burned skin.
A voice emerged. It was the voice we shared.
Now we could listen. Now we were prepared.

The Thirties

It was the Thirties once again. Shop doors
opened on hunger and long queues for soup,
the poor, clothed by the same half-empty stores,

stood round in doorways in a ragged group;
the unemployed were drunk in railway stations,
rumours of war played on a constant loop.

The Furies were running out of patience
reduced to muttering curses and the lost
were lost in their own preoccupations.

In feral offices, the running cost
of living was calculated down to pence
by those who needed least and owned the most.

Imperial glamour was the last defence.
The cinema played all-out games of doom
on borrowed power. Even our dreams were dense,

crowding us out of every empty room.
We threw each other out for lack of rent
We were the bust remains of what was boom.

And knowing this, that none of it was meant,
not quite precisely as the world turned out
but as a fanciful presentiment,

was of no consolation. None could doubt
what was happening. The sea was emptiness
out of which light emerged. One distant shout

and it was here, the water's fancy dress
of time as tide, the crowds along the street
jostling to hear a demagogue's address.

Where else was all the troubled world to meet?
Why was the water rushing to the door?
At whose damp walls were the loud waves to beat?

Blessed Isle

(for Alvin Pang)

1 *Sling*

They are spreading the wealth.
You can see it glow for miles.
It is the jewelled sandwich, the pearl cocktail.
The food that is everywhere abundant.

Look into the eye of the storm.
There the lightning flashes.
It too is brilliant. It blurs, illuminates,
washes out, and kills.

2 *Complication*

The small scurry down the street,
blown along by the rain,
the voided clouds.

The heat outside is
almost one with the heat inside.
We bring it with us.

It is hard to know
what scale of being
inhabits us.

We expand in lights
and miles of reclaimed land.
We watch storms come and go.

We are inhabited
by enormous skies.
It is complicated.

3 *An Open Book*

Intelligence here is anxiety. Where is it not?
We dare not break hearts for fear of making noise.
Such noise is vulgar. We watch skies clot
and darken. We're cool with that. The boys
are at their desks. The girls darken and strut.
Now the books are open. Now they're shut.

4 *Solo for slam*

I am not air. I am skin. I am
a voice practising to be naked.
I stomp and hurl myself at you.

I declaim what is normally whispered.
I am how I say and how I scream it.
I am the implicit that's explicit.

I am the insect on the glass.
I am the leaf you are obliged to break.
I am the pain at the back of your eye.

This is my new model of catharsis.
This is my volume, skin, air, flesh.
I am already among you.

5 *Slogan*

You voted for it last time round: you'll vote for it again.
You can soak it in for decades and never worry about
effects. It's part of the courteous way things shout
at you without barking. Now you can watch that stain
of cloud darken. It might or might not come to thunder.
The climate is stable. There's no such thing as winter.

6 *Monsoon*

The thunder rolls down
the hill of its own breathing.
The darkness stiffens.

If you stay still now
it will ignore you. Lightning
will pass over you.

Thunder's argument
is with someone else.
It is someone else's voice.

There is another
presence in the darkness. Look
into its blind eyes.

They look beyond you
into a space so boundless
a voice can echo

for ever. Tiny
selves of rain, tongues of lost mouths,
sharp teeth of thunder,

and a deep stomach
that is part voice, part burning,
all are gathered there.

Breath, density, light...
Thunder knows their names, and yours
but will pass over.

Thunder won't call you
in from the rain or meet you
at your open door.

It's not meant for you.
Thunder has priorities.
You're not one of them,

but it lives in you
as if you were the echo
blowing itself out.

7 *Dance*

You don't want the dollar, you wan't papaya,
papaya free, singing and dancing, live,
juiced up, imbecilic, impeccable, grave,
ambassadorial, warm-hearted. You want fire
and the big sea, you want grieved and young,
or so she sang of death in her own tongue.

8 *Melancholy as fruit*

You could buy it all
and still be short of something
like, say, papaya.

I am thinking now
of a terminal sweetness,
I'm thinking of love,

and the sensory realm
love brings us. It is language.
It is what you miss

without papaya
or without guava, without
the cold sweet phonemes

of whatever word
denotes the mysterious
weeping you can hear.

9 *Blessed Isle*

It was happy and kind. It was the land
of amenable souls. It did things just right
and continued doing so. But late at night
energies took their fill. Each hand
wielded an imagined axe. The sea was high
in the bay. The malls were running dry.

10 *Fragmentary*

I write in fragments
he wrote. Life is fragmented.
This too is fragment.

The clouds built and broke
into ever softer chunks
of light, deep fragments

like an unwritten
sentence waiting for ever
to be completed.

You could hear laughter
or the song of unseen birds
engaged then parting.

We should complete them.
We should end our sentences.
We should make good sense

of all of this. Yes,
but that would mean completing
thoughts, thoughts that refuse to

settle in the mind.
Which is where we are now. Here,
wherever this is,

which is several
places at once. We must work
harder. We must stop.

11 *A place where*

You could cut the air with a knife yet it is soft
as a feather pillow. You could eat away your life
yet be afraid of the dark. You could happily drift
through the street. You could contemplate grief
like an organism through the microscope
of your bank account and still retain some hope.

Postcolonial Operations

September. Morning.
Here the peaceable kingdom,
pale and serious.

Foreign languages
blossom in corners. Far off
bright blooms. Acts of speech.

On the hot island
food is served, chairs are wiped down,
nation building starts.

One think of angels
at their impossible angles
slippcd into language.

Between languages
the hot day explains itself
using simple terms.

Puritans close down
the cinema of the soul,
yelling at the light.

Into September.
Into crispness. Into evening.
Into the clock's face.

Back to the empire.
Back to old rites of passage.
Late sun. Darkness. Song.

Patriarchs

You see them perched in a row on a beam
high above the city. They have no harness,
no safety rail. They are munching sandwiches
prepared by their wives sixty storeys below
or bought at an early morning stall. From there
they survey the world like gods without power,
like flightless sparrows or shreds of windblown paper.
At school, when asked about careers, they answered:
this, this girder, this vertiginous height, this pay,
this beer, these sandwiches, are what we aspire to,
life being short, and frequently shorter,
occasionally abrupt and always dangerous. This pride
is what we master, this mustering of self and air,
this, and fatherhood or livelihood, the fight
in the bar or the alley, the triumph or disaster
of a joke told to gods on the same high beam.
We're born for this, to this, it is our station
and pride, our working principle. The foreman
strides among us, the boss approves the plans,
the food appears on our plates. It is our domain.
It is the urban wind that blows between streets
that are yet to rise to their full stature. We hang
between floors like decorations, a rank of medals
strung to a ragged chest. It is our choice. We make it.

Then they descend, one by one, along more beams,
down steps, resisting gravity, as they're obliged to.

After a line of W.H. Auden

About suffering the old bastards
    were very seldom wrong,
turning our flesh to dust so we might turn
    that dust to song,
their own songs being the kind to which we
     were obliged to sing along.

In Defence of Cliché

Man at a Bar

We negotiate
the barren rocks of cliché,
steering by cliché.

Rocks, whirlpools, sandbanks:
the metaphors are themselves
insecure symbols.

Of course the sea, yes,
the undertow, yes, the drag
of the tide, the swell

of something valid
and painful and terrible,
yes, and we mean it.

See, there is the bar,
a man is leaning on it,
there are his red eyes.

And there on the floor
something slips from his pocket,
an object so small

it seems unlikely
to be a metaphor for
anything. He's drunk.

He is muttering
clichés to himself. He slurs
his words, and the sea

is rising round him,
up to his waist now, rising.
This too is cliché.

We are never there.
Never precisely. He is
dreaming of symbols.

In Defence of Cliché

He talked in clichés
because he could at least talk
when talking was hard.

He talked of his loss,
of his 'angel', his 'sunshine'
'the light of his life'.

Clichés were his tongue
and his heart, his whole being
in that wild moment.

The articulate
could choose their words carefully
and make distinctions

but for him there were
no suitable distinctions.
Nothing was distinct

except the difference
between loss and its numbness
which was not language.

So he spoke clichés
he had learned without learning,
just as one learns pain

of which there's plenty
that never does stop talking,
rocking to and fro

as the voiceless do
and the child, being instinct
with its wordlessness,

a silent cliché,
a gentleness of dead words
in search of the dead.

What we talk about when we talk about talking

Some talk about things,
some talk about other things,
some about people.

Some don't talk at all
but pull faces and pretend
to listen not talk.

Some are trapped inside
an empty conversation
and can't quite get out.

See that young man there?
Watch his mouth move. Watch his hands
as he tries to speak.

Something must be said
but it escapes him before
he knows what it is.

Something fugitive
is in the forsaken air
before its saying.

Pity the speechless
with their gesticulation
and their stiff white lips.

Where's the oxygen
of publicity now? Choked
off. Gone for a walk.

Some talk about things.
Some don't talk at all. Talking
is this. This is talk.

Insomnia

The way he sits there
you can see he hasn't slept.
His eyes keep shifting.

Behind him a man
is reading from a tablet,
working at figures.

By the wide window
a woman picks at her food
and reads the paper.

But his eyes are lost
in their own restless orbit
moving like space junk.

Nothing to see here.
No reassuring planet
to be discovered.

Outside it's raining.
The town is packed with shoppers.
The streets are dark grey.

Nothing in the eyes
except panic. Nothing but
the desire to leave.

And nothing occurs.
The rain continues to fall.
People read and eat.

Here is where we live.
Here is our planet of streets
and tables and chairs.

This is our space junk.
This is our winter weather.
These are our tables.

Assault

They were kicking him
for no specific reason.
They simply kicked him.

It took five minutes,
the girls standing by, watching.
The street was quiet.

It wasn't fatal.
He wasn't badly injured.
Nothing had broken.

The leaves turned and tossed
a little in the light breeze.
A car was passing.

There would be bruises
and possibly the police
who would be helpful.

Spleen
(after Baudelaire)

I'm like the king of a rainy country, rich
but wobbly kneed, both cub and toothless bitch.
I'm through with books, and poems and string quartets;
I've sold the horses, shot the household pets.
Cheer up? Not likely, board games are a bore
and as for 'the people' dying by my door,
fuck them, and fuck that guitar-wielding clown,
who's worse than useless when I'm feeling down.
See, here I am, full length, stuck in my bed,
the girls can put on sex shows, give me head,
go girl on girl, no point, it just won't work,
it won't jump-start this junky royal jerk.
The quack who brings me pills and knows a trick
to harden flaccid aristocratic dick,
may as well bring blood and the Roman Baths,
the kind that suited those old psychopaths.
No good, I'm dead in muscle, nerve, and brain.
It's all green Lethe and that bloody rain.

The Boy-King's Tale

Off with his head, screamed the queen. And his. And his. And that other one's. I don't trust heads. I don't like your nose.

The boy at the queen's side took out his catapult and shot the man's nose off. It was his first act in the dynasty.

The space where the man's nose had been was a vacancy that should have been filled. A man without a nose is an offence, said the queen.

The queen died. The noseless man's head was impaled on a pole. All was well in the kingdom now the boy was on the throne.

The ghost of the noseless man hovered around the palace corridors. The boy-king had it arrested for nothing less than treason.

The generals of the army all had noses but some noses were bigger than others. A degree of consistency was required.

All the generals were sheared of their noses by royal order. Their faces were an offence to the boy-king. He sheared them of their heads.

More ghosts crowded the palace. The boy-king had them arrested. His catapult became the state emblem, vert on gules.

The people are hungry, reported the cowering messenger. The boy-prince sheared off his nose then his head. Feed them to the people, he said.

The people rose against the boy-king. He had them arrested and decapitated. My people are ghosts, he said to no one in particular.

Laughter

7 January 2015

So they set out to kill the laughter. They wore
death as if God had been committed to their unique
and tender care. No one should laugh again, they swore.
But laughter comes when it will and is strong, not weak.

Meet Harpo

Talking to Groucho
wasn't easy. He would roll
his big eyes and sneer.

Talking to Chico
was no easier. His fake
accent took over.

Talking to Harpo
was like talking to a blast
of angry white air.

They were familiars
not people. I knew them all
as shapes in dead fire.

Above all Harpo,
explosive, a child with fits
of terrible greed.

Outside in the storm
the brothers were blown along
ravines and high seas.

Everyone scattered
in the wind. It was wartime.
It was rationing.

Dread sister, Laughter,
have you no care for brothers
of thunderous talk?

Beware the silent
speechifier in the wig.
Cross your legs. Fight back.

In the Country of the Heart

I couldn't remember if I had left my heart in the right place. There is a place for everything.

My heart was on a train heading for the right place but would it get there on time?

My heart was in one of two places, neither of them right.

Must you talk about your heart, they asked. We'll be the judges of that.

They were looking into my mouth but it was my heart they were looking for so I produced a heart for them.

Is this your heart, they asked. You don't want to leave it lying about the place.

May we direct you to the right place for your heart, they asked, indicating their batons.

I was able to demonstrate that my heart was in the right place. That seemed to satisfy them.

All our hearts were in the right place. It was getting crowded in there.

Too many hearts in one place. We were having trouble orientating ourselves.

Our hearts were joined in one big heart. Our hearts were full to overflowing.

My eyes were closed, my mouth was wide open and shouting, my liver had gone missing, but my heart was in the right place.

Minimalist

The minimal is the intense, says one
whose life has been chopped small and rarely done,
a little steak, a little blood, a gun.

The minimal is terrible. The parts
you amputated vanish: nothing charts
their painful absence. Nothing stops or starts.

Eliminating waste, the minimal
is what remains. You call it seminal,
but it is bare. Excess is criminal.

So this is tiny. Life, alas, is short.
You don't need a cast of thousands for support.
Cut down. Relax. It's blood. Enjoy the sport.

Charge Sheet

That is not a man.
That is a thinking machine
with eyes and fingers.

Look at him working.
He's doing nothing useful.
Those are only words.

Do words shift the load
hanging by a thread or turn
a key in the door?

Do words perform tasks
that address the rain and clouds?
Some of us doubt it.

Words have no substance.
They hang around street corners,
menacing shadows

waiting for something
to happen so they may spread
like an infection.

They take up the air
the useful need to function.
We do not need them.

They should let us be
and amuse themselves elsewhere
on some distant moon.

The doors are open.
Out there is light and silence.
Let the silence come.

When the wicked come...

They will be polite
and carry badges of proof
so you should know them.

They'll be precisely
what you expect, conformist
in all their dealings.

You may welcome them
in your own symbolic way,
whatever that is.

You may gnash your teeth
if that is your preference.
The wicked won't mind.

Avoiding mirrors
is their preference. They will
let you look in yours.

They will be correct
according to their custom
which is time-honoured.

They will wreak havoc
then shrug and apologise
for all they have done.

Let the wicked come.
They can't stand there for ever
knocking at the door.

They can't help their state.
Invite them in. Sit them down.
Let them wreck your life.

There, that wasn't hard.
Wicked is as wicked does.
We all do something.

Eden

We carry strangeness
in our blood. We are outcasts
from our own Eden.

Eden is elsewhere.
That is its definition,
he explains, smiling.

Not that this helps us.
Not that knowledge of Eden
makes Eden a place.

Nothing of Eden
remains except memory,
which is not a place.

Outside, the fury.
Outside, the storm in the waste
and the rage of dust.

He says this smiling:
he refuses to console
except by smiling.

He invites us on
to consider our options,
if we have options.

We have dust and smiles.
We have rage within Eden.
These are our options.

There will be trouble,
he says, smiling. What to do
but smile and talk on?

We rise from our chairs.
They take the coffee away.
We pay, smile, and part.

In his smile, agony.
In his calm, uncertainty.
Nothing in his hands.

Minimenta: A Topography

(for Anselm Kiefer)

The topography of ruins. One wave
of grass covers everything. I have seen
a woman bending over a stone.
Everything around her was green.

The desire is to leave everything alone.
The difficulty is knowing what to save.

*

I am a wreck, says one, but not
with his mouth. Where are his organs
of speech? They've been wrecked
by the huge wind that blows, now hot
now cold. Too late to protect
a body fraying at the margins.

*

The smallest things move me. The rain
as it shakes the leaf. The sound of laughter
in the street. I'm easy to please.
Give me fine particulars, he says,
the microfiction of pleasure. A train
passing. The silence after.

*

Somewhere within his chest
a crow was croaking. Somewhere not far
from him bodies were decomposing.
Everything in the world was for the best.
Outside leaves lifted. The sky was closing
round a tree on a distant star.

*

44

The terrain of grief does not grow any smaller.
The bush fires spread. The dead keep interrupting.
A crowd shouting in the park meets a crowd
shouting in the street. Shouting turns to shooting.
Turn off the film. The soundtrack is too loud.
We don't need sound. We don't need technicolour.

*

But here is colour: hands, eyes and lips,
magnified as if for real, then vanishing
into the sinkholes that punctuate
the landscape.
             I don't say anything,
says the mouth. *You are too late,*
say the eyes, hands, and fingertips.

*

You build ruins we can live in.
You hide our bones in concrete.
The bomb shelter is inside the bomb.

Here is the car we arrive in.
Here is what remains of the street.
Here it all stops. Welcome home.

A Drunken Boat

The Drunken Boat

Bring me the boy. Let me make of him
a small god of impatience. Let him scream
and roll his eyes as in the dream
of his own apotheosis in the fire
he builds for himself. Let him aspire
to perfection in his own kingdom.

He will be precocious certainly.
His gifts will be spectacular. His mouth
will be a receptacle for alchemical truth.
His teeth will burn, his brows become
a script in old books of spells, the sum
of wisdoms beyond the guff of poetry.

That violet gaze must be intoxicating
to all who meet it. Let him pour down his throat
as much drink as he needs for his drunken boat
so he might explore the exotic savages of the land
he imagines, and all the contraband
of sobersides who are there for the taking.

Slum

The poor are always stinking up the place
so drag in the rich, their majesties, his grace.

The foul in doorways with their foul dogs sleep
in other doorways, four, five bodies deep.

How Napoleonic it all is. The wreck of hope
embodied in sleek fashion and old rope.

Boy genius, we welcome your contempt.
Drive out the wicked and remain unkempt.

Lecture your masters. Seduce them. Point your tongue
at the great. Don't let them go unsung.

Conneries

A sharp priapic tongue. You wiggle it.
What else are you to do with it?
What is your tongue for? Don't ask
because you know already, don't you?
It is a wild tongue as all tongues are
but not everyone will be licking
into those corners.

   Somewhere in a dark suburban room
the demons are biting each others' tongues.
Let's join them! Let there be no more tongues
only their lodgings and lodgements.

Let there be bullets and broadsides,
a long voyage down the world's throat.

Royal Street

Any street might wake to find itself possessed
by demons fully dressed,
such as Verlaine and Rimbaud, innocent enough
to look at but both rough,
both poets, one delicately corrosive
the other explosive.

Welcome to London, demons, this is Doré's patch
ready to burn at the striking of a match.
Let's set it briefly alight and make of it a game
of fury, lighting an alcoholic flame.
Sometimes we need to burn as from within:
so conflagrations begin.

In the City

In the city a street
in the street a house
in the house a room
that keeps opening
on a scene at the heart
of which is a meeting
where what is impossible
meets the ridiculous
in a possible city
while rain falls gently
almost languorously
all but seductively
on a man trudging home
from market to a door
in the house up the stairs
to the room where
something is closing
and yet remains open
open as a gutter
open as Africa
open as the future
which is modern and dying.

At the Corner of the Table

You don't even have to look at the painting. You see
them there, the young Rimbaud, head ablaze with hair,
the older Verlaine somehow cramped, tightly gripping the glass
of wine before him. It is a minute before midnight
in the history of the moment. We know where this is going,
we have known from the start. It is there in the light,
in the way a row of solemn figures determinedly pass
before a pair of eyes not in control of their knowing.
The poets know this is not quite a private affair
but a public moment launched into posterity.

How to return from a past that is already on fire? How to turn
from a line that will not turn? How to open monstrous
beauty up to dissection? Something is moving amongst us.
We don't see the fire leap but know how it will burn.

Prudence

Et je hais toujours la femme jolie,
La rime assonante et l'ami prudent.

PAUL VERLAINE, 'Résignation'

Hating assonance as also prudence he dreamt
of endless harems and *paradis physiques*
which are all that are left to the weak.

He loved the distances with scent enough to tempt
the imagination with Heliogabalus and more,
a fleshly brilliant gem, a Koh-i-Noor.

He hated prudence and was through with rhyme.
Assonance was for ninnies. So he ran away
with a boy like a slut he didn't have to pay
who was cruel and childish and sublime.

It's what all children want beyond the breast
of mothers you can rely on and deserve.
You ride the luxuriant ship of the female curve
until your phallic sun finally sinks in the west.

City Snapshots

1

Always hoping to open yet another hole
in himself so that something utterly new
might crawl out and blaze like the soul
at the bottom of poems, visible through
the smoke of a city black as coal
and as full of evil as a man might do
given the chance, he let the poem stroll
nonchalantly down the tree-lined avenue.

2

At seventeen your hand is sweaty and unpleasant,
a dreadful object you must carry with you
unless you tuck it into your pocket and whistle a tune,
almost any tune as long as you are whistling,
as long as your hands remain in your pockets
where they may remain as they are, sweaty and unpleasant.

3

Entering the station the ground falls away
the earth moves, the great engines of the mind
gather steam and begin to move out beyond
the city into a notional comfort where the blind
corners and myopic alleys of the village stray
off into vacancies: the inn, the village pond,
whatever you call nature or the authorities
define as nature as required by powerful cities.

4

Cast off responsibilities and taste the last
winter in your blood. I don't know what that means
but I believe in it. That is what the holy text
instructs us to do. Believe. And so we fast
or indulge, it doesn't matter which. It is the next
thing you do which is forever beyond your means.

5

Song is acid thrown into your face. It should
take the skin off. Paint peels, bricks soften.
London's the melting pot in which you melt.
Make your visit now and come back often.

6

All those endless suburbs that extend
into the stubborn country. We belong
in the rain. We walk past excavations.
We fall foul of ourselves everywhere.
These are the *grands projets* of ourselves.
It's where we live, the strangely familiar air.

7

From the window you can look down
the entire length of the street. You can see
who is coming. You can sit on the ledge
and kick out. This is the heart of town
for now, the deep heart of the world
you inhabit but it's also the world's edge.

8

At the foot of dark walls beating the skinny dogs.
My poor heart dribbles at the stern. You note
the visceral smear on your fingertips. You revise
the text of your disgust. You disown what you wrote.
You become *another*, leaving your lyrical dregs
to your ruined friend, to those whom you despise.

9

Memory memory, what do you want? I recall
the walks through gardens, the great park
where the blackbird's song pirouetted and sprang
into air, where her white hand set off the dark
of the trees while the nearby chuchbells rang
me into being and death. And that is all.

10

De la douceur. Of sweets too much.
The heart, *couvert de caporal*,
leaves the city, lights the match,
remains merely corporeal.
Something bursts. A paper bag
and life proceeds from rag to rag.

Bruno Schulz, She Said

I no longer know
the difference between nightmare
and dreaming, she said.

Almost everything
I see in dreams frightens me,
she said. It was dark.

Most wonderful things –
doors that open on heaven –
remain dark, she said.

I would like to wake
at a moment of brightness,
unafraid, she said.

It's all parody,
echo of echo, she said.
I can't hear things straight.

I've met Bruno Schulz.
He sleeps in my bed, she said,
though I can't see him.

Schulz is just a name
I can't get out of my head,
like music, she said.

And so she talked on,
changing genders now and then,
telling me her dreams.

But I couldn't say
what the difference was myself.
I too was dreaming.

We were together
in this. She kept on talking.
It was a long night.

On Angels

In derelict streets
full of blind houses the eyes
are shattered windows.

When the blind windows
open their eyes they will see.
Their gods will listen.

Here's the high gable.
Here come the angels, all eyes
and ears and trumpets.

The blind shall open
their eyes and the dumb shall speak,
proclaim the trumpets.

Angels are fallen.
Look at the vacant spaces.
See, they are massing.

Out of the bare street
emerges the thin angel
they've been harbouring.

Its enormous wings
extend either side of it
casting vast shadows.

Here is where we live,
the streets declare. These sad walls
are our one defence.

Nor is there an hour
without angels. They become
what the street breathes out.

Here is where we live:
in the breathing of the street,
among the trumpets.

Nine Meditations on Francesca Woodman

1

The self tends to squat
in awkward positions so
it might see itself.

2

Frail, vulnerable,
exposed. Even fully clothed
one remains naked.

3

Image rehearses
its positions. Nothing
detains an image.

4

Nakedness becomes
an explanation. Nothing
is explained thereby.

5

Sheets of clear plastic,
rooms blown clear of the body,
sculpture as sculpture.

6

Body as stop-frame
animation. So the frame
stops. So body stops.

7

Body as nude. Dead
phrases gathered into speech,
the tongue's slick grammar.

8

We are never where
we might be. We are statues
of complete absence.

9

Everywhere too much.
Everything as metaphor.
Except this. Not this.

Like That Raw Engine

Like placing a stone
in the dead centre of night,
a hard lightless sun.

Like falling from day
into an electric pool
of unlit currents.

Like horizontal.
Like fish alive on a slab.
Like breathing. Like light.

Like a parallel
existence. Like another.
Like something else here.

Like the rain in dreams
only absent. Like the rain
in life still falling.

Like a distant car
moving towards you. Like that.
Like that raw engine.

Like time in darkness,
undetectable, hanging,
uncertain yet clear.

To sing what is 'like'.
To talk into parallels.
To think like water.

Speak into silence.
Who listens as intently?
Who answers? Who wakes?

And the night opens
its hands and gives you something:
a gift of plain tongues.

Jukebox

A Hard Day's Night

From the first chord we knew what we had lost.
The old landscape was re-adjusting its dress
but not to cover up the old distress.
Nothing was predictable. We had crossed
some threshhold and had emerged into a place
that was ourselves but otherwise. The noise
itself was new. It strutted a new poise
with a new haircut and a different face.

We launched out into a world devoid of guilt.
No army discipline now, war was done.
Our fathers were older and our mothers' bruised.
Both looked away. Everything they had built
was ours now. The old rules were confused,
as was apparent once we had begun.

Island of Dreams

On the island of dreams a woman with solid hair
is flanked by two handsome custodians.
I fall in love. It's that firm halo of hers
that fascinates me. I fall in love with her voice,
her eye-shadow, with the frailty implicit in her gloss.
Suddenly I'm in a bedroom, the occupier elsewhere,
being perfect, since perfection always occurs
elsewhere, in a street, at the tip of a nose,
in a voice beyond itself located inside a mouth,
and it is her mouth that leaves me with no choice
but to love and desire. It is not precisely youth
that grabs me but the island of dreams, the loss
of that solid hair, the warm breath that hangs
about her, and the velvet of her lungs.

Sealed with a Kiss

We were always beautiful. Always. When we wrote
each other it was our beauty we were committing
to paper, a beauty composed of forgetting.
It was beauty that caught us, that set us afloat
on the great painted sea of our disasters.
It was beauty that moved us against the tide
of dead water, that slowly pushed us aside
and beached us. Here we met the masters
of our fortunes: time, separation, space
with its inevitable music, the lost boys
of the movies, the sweatered girls, the slow
ring of dancers moving to white noise;
the simple sadness of the hand and face,
the loss of the sealed kiss, the long hard blow.

Needle in a Haystack

We were never quite good enough at it,
or *for* it, that love extended to us
by the soft arms of unearned merit.
And then it goes: the sparkling, glamorous
invitations fail, all that we yearn for,
she in her summer dress in the garden, gone
indoors to remain behind a closed door,
changing her bright outfit, putting on
a cardigan fit for autumn. So others go
doing their simple vanishing act and once
they vanish it is worse than trying to find
a needle in that haystack. You are blind
enough as it is, child. The rest is chance,
but look to prick yourself. You never know.

You've Lost That Loving Feeling

When that deep voice rises from the bottom
of your chest it is like a warning. Do not
attack Cuba, miss out on the fatal shot
in Dallas, observe the holding pattern
of clouds, preserve the secret of your success
behind your chiselled features. Let us learn
the trouble of deep waters and follow the stern
laws of the republic. Let us wear the dress
of sorrow with a certain elegance. It is time
we learned to react to the loss of love.
It's time for gravity. Let the darkness move
through your voice like gravel, let it climb
into its own echo. Sing to us. Wait
for your cue. Go now, before it's too late.

Shine On You Crazy Diamond

And so they shone, every one of them,
each crazy, everyone a diamond shining
the way things shine, each becoming a gleam
in his own eyes, deep in the satin lining
of their own jackets, and it was no dream
just a momentary forgetfulness, a nothing
like nothing on earth: Apollinaire's diadem,
a star-shaped, sudden, silent mouthing.

And they were there, vanished as if for ever.
And we were there and saw them in the flesh
with skeletal faces, their hair in long rivers
of black, their eyes deep coals and ash,
and this was memory or its imagining,
ourselves as light as if for ever spinning.

Nowhere to Run

In the Detroit assembly plant men are spraying paint
while Martha and the girls run around as though it were
a playground. No paint is going to get on her.
It's an amusement park. No one lodges a complaint
about them, there are no safety issues at stake.
Work can be fun in Motown. Component parts
float past, doors, hoods, the whole process starts
and finishes here with this song, all in one take.
Nowhere to hide, she sings but there are countless places
one might shelter behind for a moment or so,
and then it all moves forward again, past the faces
at their tasks, past the girls themselves,
and here we are in ghost town, ready to go
and when you've gone the whole city dissolves.

In Wolf's Clothing

The Wolf Reader

(for Marilyn Hacker)

There were the books and wolves were in the books.
They roamed between the words. They snarled and loped
through stories with bedraggled wolfish looks

at which the hackles rose and the world stopped
in horror, and she read them since she knew
the pleasures of reading, as the page was rapt

with the magic of the fierce, and she could do
the voices of such creatures. So one day
when teacher asked if there were any who

could read, she rose as if the task were play,
to claim the story where she felt at home.
The tale was Riding Hood, the wolf was grey.

The fierceness was the wood where grey wolves roam.
She read it round, she read it through and through
It was as if the wolf were hers to comb,

like those bedraggled creatures in the zoo,
that trapped behind the bars would snarl and stride
as you'd expect a page or wolf to do.

A Paradise Garden

1

And so I had to find them: fish and birds
among the strands of living lineations
in which the world was elegantly tangled.
It was all I could do with my limited store of words.
The ropes we weave are the ropes by which we're strangled.
The lines we draw are the ones that snap our patience.

It was arrow and shower homing in on me
swooping like gulls over the breaking waves,
that landscape of pure water running loose.
I wish I were as straight as a young tree.
I wish I were as taut as that light noose.
I wish it were neat pins that marked our graves.

2

See, here those perfect circles of pure light
define a space within the mind. See, there
those arcs of grey a steady hand may hold
to a true rhythm, how they pitch, take flight,
and dip again. It's as if world could fold
in on itself and leave a gap in air.

We learn by moving. So the hand that weaves
the curious pattern where a dancer moves.
We stream in on the rhythms of the blood
as it circulates. We tremble like the leaves
in terror when the steep wind is in flood.
We're what we feel and what our logic proves.

3

Deeper within the folds of our inner skin,
those guttural and labial caverns crushed
into viscera, we find new creatures lost
to the outer world: the curious pangolin,
the eccentric hummingbird, all the crossed
breeds of the imagination, brushed

and smeared across a hard wall in the dark.
It's where we live. Lit by the lightning jags
of neural weather we stumble as best we can
over terrain where reason leaves a mark
by which we identify the place as human
complete with its trail of bones and flints and rags.

Among Animals

Touch the animals
in your head. They bend to you
gently as to food.

They shuffle along
from ark to ark, obedient
as your own shadow.

You feed the creatures
with the pity they inspire,
your imagined tribe.

The domestic cat
that winds its body round you
and lives in your throat.

The tame dog you feed
that is your several limbs
and your lifted head.

And all the wild beasts
in your eyes. What will you do
with them while you sleep?

Here's the stuffed giraffe
of your childhood, its long neck.
Here is its faint smile.

Here is the caged bird
you spent such hours talking to.
Will it now talk back?

The inhabitants
of your body have gathered
in herds to hear you.

What will you say now
your languages have failed you
and your eyes are lost?

Creatures construct you.
The world put you together
as its quaint puzzle.

Now you dismantle
the night. Now you call the dark
to its vast kennel.

Your territory
is crowded with animals
that go their own ways.

Behold your creatures,
says the book of the body.
Converse with your tribe.

Animal Inside

It was as if I were trying to climb into its eyes
or mouth, the animal that inhabited me,
as if I could take myself by surprise

and rid my body of what I couldn't see.
If my zoo was open and supplied with creatures
that might be exhibited without a fee

it was because I had yielded to their natures
and we were one and always had been so.
I had even inherited some of their better features:

the eyes I entered, the mouth through which could flow
the speech I knew. The public could explore
our habitat and know what they couldn't know

without a frank display. But still I wanted more,
I wanted the beast that spoke, the mind that sprang
to such attention and yet somehow ignore

the most essential things that should belong
to consciousness, the kind that I possessed.
I was a hollow thing and yet my body rang

with presence and the feeling left me stressed
and oddly naked despite my clothes because
this was public and I was underdressed.

My animals were with me. I watched their paws
pad lightly across the floor to enter me
as gently as they could, with soft retracted claws.

Their silence sat inside me, the cacophony
that they called language had resolved to sense
of a sort but lacked a reliable dictionary.

I was lost. This *we*, this *us*, this curious pretence
of peaceable kingdoms was coming to an end.
I should say something but have no defence.

Blakesongs

The Ghost of a Flea

In 12-12-5

Call Dürer's rhino and Blake's flea to order.
Let animals enter the kingdom through the eye
            and lodge in the mind.
The imagination is feasible. Go there.
Inhabit the jungle of the long comfortless
            night of the spirit.

Everything that lives is holy. The swatted fly
continues to buzz in the glass with its motor
            running. The machine
of the body starts up as images enter
its cavities. The lamb lies down with the lion
            in the haunted fold.

The ghost of the flea is a ghost in paradise.
The sacred spaces are inhabited. The dream
            of the numinous
continues into day. We will be prophets. We
will live with our ghosts. We created them
            now they sleep with us.

Here comes the flea, hopping from bed to bed. Here
is the rhinoceros entering the sheepfold.
            Someone calls them home
and sets them dancing across the luminous page
of the holy. We welcome them with provisos.
            They are our children.

A Vision of the Daughters of Albion

Thy soft American plains are mine, and mine thy north & south

So it was regarding the daughter with her soft plains
and other softness of the traditional kind
that had, it is written, set fire to both Troy and the plains.

She was, after all, an amorous image generated in the folds
of the curtain by a youth shut up in his chamber. His pillow
was silent and his mind burned throughout its generous folds.

Elsewhere, on a screen, in full real-time action, her body was deployed
in a variety of ways by a variety seeking ever more varieties.
The body is soon burned away unless it is deployed.

This being America, a land new found by some, though old enough
to those who inhabited her, the pioneer spirit cried out against
continence and its meaner rewards. Nothing would be enough.

The womb of enormous joys is opened unto itself. World enters
its joys with religious fervour out of horrible darkness.
The daughters of joy entertain the violent in whatever form it enters.

From north, from south, they arrive, stampt with their signet. They come
at the moment of desire, that endlessly recurring moment. They pine
and appear, they make their entrance, they come and go and come.

The plains are burning. The daughters burn. The youth burns with his curtain
in the blaze of his lungs. The terrors observe at the door. Their business
is burning. Their fierce desire is the scourge in the folds of the curtain.

Nurse's Song

When voices of children are heard on the green

The dews of night arise.
The house is still. It is late
to be out. The sky hangs above us
like a monumental weight.

And then a child's voice
clear as the sky, pure as the bird
in its dark nest. The brief song
of what happens. The word.

The Sick Rose

O rose thou art sick!

There is love-sickness and being sick
to the stomach, but why the sickness?
Why the invisibility? Why the rose
dying as if love were poison?

My joy was crimson, the rose answers,
but then came the storm. My bed
was no bed of roses. The sickness
is in the soil and in the air.

Why ask about the worm? Why blame
love for what happens to the rose?
Then a great blast of wind shakes
the petals. Then the yearning.

Nine Annotations to *The Proverbs of Hell*

Dip him in the river who loves water

Drive your cart and your plow over the bones of the dead

He drove his cart too well, the furrows ran
with the blood of angels and the blood of man.
He thought the field was bothersome with stones
but it was bones. Dry bones.

The road of excess leads to the palace of wisdom

This is the palace of wisdom. Note the marble
staircase and the exquisite carpets looted from Ispahan.
This is the presidential suite. The road of excess
leads here. No map needed. You have the address.

Prudence is a rich ugly old maid courted by Incapacity

I knew Prudence. She was
pretty once and fierce as hell.
I am not exactly Incapacity
but as good as, and will do as well.

Bring out number weight & measure in a year of dearth

Make your offerings here as an act of charity.
We live in dearth or else austerity.
Dip your hands in your pockets. It won't hurt you
to practise a little individual virtue.

Prisons are built with stones of Law, Brothels with bricks of Religion

Our prophet demands we cover up your neck
but let us compound that with your nose and eyes
lest any feel the least desire to flirt.
At home the blind will gladly raise that skirt.

One thought, fills immensity

It's how you keep thinking, as if fury were a thought.
This is the universe, the immensity we bought.

The tygers of wrath are wiser than the horses of instruction

The heady days of Paris and all those horses
instructing their tygers in the usual courses.
Wisdom is guns or else these burning eyes.
Now imitate the action of the wise!

Damn, braces: Bless relaxes

Chill out, you're doing fine. Let's see your smiling faces.
Relax, dear souls. Unwind. Undo those awful braces.

Sooner murder an infant in its cradle than nurse unacted desires

There is no current shortage of murdered infants.
Come to think of it there rarely is a dearth.
Desire must blaze its path and we must follow.
We are desirable from infancy. From birth.

Courtship

Courtship

One dreams of feathers,
another of eggs and wings,
another of nests.

Some dream of flying,
some of rising from the ground
just an inch or two.

There are rituals
enacted in dizzy air
between earth and sky.

The infinite care
of the act, the hovering
involved, the desire

and the becoming,
the sheer breasting of the air,
the leaning on it.

Is this how love burns,
shimmering in its feathers,
looking to touch down?

Is there a landing
that is all but permanent,
some cry or scuffle

of claw and feather,
small beaks gaping in branches,
then the urge to fly?

We have heard them mourn,
hidden in the trees, a trill
or distant chatter.

Open up the air
and there's the beating of wings,
each feather alight.

On Beauty

I don't know what to do with beauty, with the curled
lip, with the delicate bones, with the cocked wrist,
with that sudden sense of being hurled

into a place I have no right to be, as if to exist
on such ground might be forbidden, allowed
only a glimpse, then what to do with it? We have missed

the last bus home. We have become detached from the crowd.
The spirit moves with the body. The mind wakes
from its dream of weightlessness. The high cloud

forms itself into fantasy. It is an act that takes
our breath away. I am awake. I lack perfection.
I am a votary of something at which the hand shakes.

Now to walk. Now to find a route through the fiction
of becoming. I know I am dying and that my time
is full of shadows, that there is no protection.

What she told me about beauty

Hard to lose beauty,
she said, and was beautiful
as she said the words.

*It is not the same
later*, she said. *Though we say
it is, it isn't.*

*And that troubles me
if only for a moment*,
she added. *How sad,*

*to consider it,
all that gradual vanishing,
all soft power gone.*

So she reflected
lost in her beautiful bones,
her beautiful mouth

moving as mouths do
in the saying of such things,
in their full moment.

*But that may be what
beauty is, the loss of it
just before the loss,*

each moment of it,
she said and took a deep breath
of plentiful air,

the air being good,
the moment just one moment,
that moment, right then.

Magic Realism

When she opened her hands the butterflies emerged
from her palms. This was the first chapter.
In the second she was speaking butterflies.
In the third her eyelids opened on butterflies.
Soon enough she would become a butterfly
since this was the story, the story behind the self
made of butterflies.
        But it was a real self,
and the butterflies too were real, there being *brimstones,*
commas, orange tips, peacocks and *painted ladies*
all of which were as real as the r*ed admirals,*
small coppers, holly blues and *grizzled skippers.*
The *mazarine* was real as was the *hairstreak,*
the *duke of burgundy*, the *grayling*, the *fritillary*,
each one of them as real as the self she was
when she wed her husband under her real name
so that the real might come into existence,
as it surely did, approaching down real streets
to a real house with real children whose real presence
grew ever more real in their own becoming real.

So the story began and I can give you detail
with time and place, complete with butterflies,
the names of the sky and of her fingernails
as written in the book of their beginning
which was as real as anything could be
that's formed to chapters and is told in words
with all those butterflies in her two hands,
those hands of hers, her palms, her mouth, her eyes.

Silver

1

It was changing in the light as such things would,
moving from pearl to lilac and beyond
to something almost murky, bottomless.
I'd dreamt it once, as one might dream of falling
from a window or high steps into a flood
of coloured darkness, bank-details, address,
all memory gone. Now it was the sound
of moonlight, a voice on the edge of calling
yet present. And so the moon appeared
in silver packaging, the shape of grief,
too dazzling while her darkened empty face
observed the world with pity close to grace.
She held our eyes then stopped and quickly sheared
off into more dark, still murkier, still brief.

2

You don't mess with the moon. Such symbols wreak
revenge, make visitations, suck the blood
from your veins. The moon taken at the flood
is what your mother thinks she is. Don't speak
ill of the moon, or her. That silver foil
is not what it seems. How many wakeful nights
have you spent under a full moon that invites
your nerves to fuse and the whole sky to boil?
Let her be cheap if she wants. Let her call
from her starry carriage. Let her complain
and vanish into you. Swallow her down
like ice-cold milk or chalk-juice. That white stain
on your brow, it's permanent however small
it looks in daylight now you're on your own.

In the Hotel Room

In the hotel room, in the dim lamplight, in her black slip,
she turned her head this way and that in the soft glow.
It was all too fragile: the darkness, the faint curve of her lip,
the slant cut of her hair, since nobody could know
just when the hard light of the corridor might burst
into that tenderest space and prove space illusion.

Whether it was his hand or the bedside light that came first
to define what she felt like, such moments of vision
were rare, with *most* blossoming suddenly out of too *little*.

It is hard being in darkness and light all at once,
to be sheltered yet vulnerable, now solid now brittle,
to be subject of both self–construction and chance.

Everything remains in its stillness while also in flight.
Love and the skin. Love and the nerves. Love, time, and night.

Overheard

That night I spent my last nickel to call Steve.
The box was empty bar the usual cards
advertising the usual services of night.
One lives for such small favours, such rewards.
One lives for what night keeps up its loose sleeve.

Steve, I said, come down. It's quite all right,
there's no one here to speak of, just a queue
waiting to get into a show and they'll be gone
once the doors open. It's just me and you.
We will be reasoned, affectionate, polite.

The stars collide and break up one by one.
The street is empty now. I've seen the show
already and it's fine. There's a decent bar
in the next block. I've seen the headlights glow
then vanish. There is nothing to be done.

So Steve came down, it wasn't very far,
and then it started raining as it does.
I felt the usual tightening in my throat.
It was the same then as it ever was.
It's what we were before. It's what we are.

Let's talk then, you and I, as if by rote.
Let us repeat the words and walk past doors
as if they weren't there and neither was the rain.
These streets and bars are our familiar shores.
But let's head out now Steve. Go get your coat.

Devious

(for Kathryn Maris)

Deviously, deviously, was he grievous and warily moping
in the something he called emptiness, which was devious,
both something and a cold, faint, lilac nothing, such as a window
or the mood he was in which was grievous and full of moping. But
this mood, this injudicious mood was his undoing, or so he considered
and said, yes said, quite clearly, while propped against the bar
in his customary fashion. It was the saying of what he was
that rendered him helpless, moving helplessly yet deviously along
the bar as he spoke shifting away beyond.... well, a
certain discomfort in the long green bar, along its metallic surface
and the words he used which continued devious and wary,
the very image of moping, the colour of the liquid
in his glass which was even then vanishing.

Illicit: A Dream Story

by way of Arthur Schnitzler

1

The mouth is cruel but the eyes are open.
The eyes drink as the mouth speaks.
The hands are busying themselves elsewhere.
This is the way things happen.
This is the way a morning breaks.
This is night. Here is the ambient air.

2

Walking at night you catch a glimpse of calf
and suddenly you are away, riding a carriage
to the enchanted mansion with its crew
of phantoms. You have failed at marriage,
you have to construct another you
to contend with. You are not your better half.

3

Who has not dreamt of a realm beyond
the provisional, a nether region where things
remain suspended for ever? You wake
in the morning and it's there before you, an ache
that is not purely light, where nothing sings,
where you touch the world and it doesn't respond.

4

Your cupidity betrays you with its puns.
You go out with a sabre fearing guns.
Your pride is flagging, whip it into shape!
You contemplate a courtship but it's rape.

You are both your own self and a slip
in language, a tongue without a lip.

5

You can turn the form round and see it
from all angles. It seems perfect does it
not? You can contain your senses in it.
What is bothering you now? What is it?
It won't let you sleep? You are hot? It
is normal. Touch yourself. You've earned it.

6

We have delved ever deeper into the psyche. Consider
the evidence. This is a brittle time. The pavement
is cracking, the walls fragile. You have no heart
to speak of. Do you insist on talking of the heart?
Do you sincerely imagine that there is pavement
under your feet? Isn't it time to reconsider?

7

The place goes mad as language. What is that noise
you keep hearing? Are people talking? Is the cafe
a hubbub of conversation? Is that a cliché
emerging from your mouth? What is that bubble
you keep blowing, the speech that annoys
and delights you? Are you well? Are you in trouble?

8

Everyone is suddenly desirable. The opposite sex
is something you dreamt up when you were unwell
one steamy night. The sexual engine is always
cruising the streets, it simply requires fuel.
You watch your fingers move and your mind stray
down a blind alley. It's not your fault. It's complex.

9

I am through with courtesy, he declared and made
a rough move which she shut off with a sweep
of her elegant hand. She touched him somewhere.
She should take off that mask. He had played
his hand, now let her play hers. It was unfair
having to play this game while half asleep.

10

Act without passion. Move your cold desire
into gear. Be vulnerable to the moon or what
stands in for moon. Betray the confidence
you promised to keep. Trust the finger-sense
that negotiates both ice and fire.
Let your eyes wander but keep your mouth shut.

11

Lie down on that couch and speak to me.
Tell me anything you want. I'm listening.
You don't know me nor do I need your name.
Let your mind roam the feral dark. Feel free
to swear. Is that your sweat glistening
in the dark? Is that shadow there your shame?

12

It's time to pack away the uniform
you've been wearing. Are you a medical man?
Is that your rank? Are those your vital
organs? This is your city. Here is the street plan
of your desire. Here is the fierce storm
of passion you've been saving. Invent a title.

Mottoes from Schnitzler

1

Talking is negotiation. Strike the deal
and go your way. Leave no grounds for appeal.

2

Innocence is a form of nagging. Lose
the pathos but be careful what you choose.

3

Sweet young bodies. See how they revolve
in the firmament. Zoom in and dissolve.

4

Cruelty is inevitable in the end.
A lover once can never be a friend.

5

What goes around comes around then goes.
The other side of your face. Your eyes. That nose.

6

Cynical? Me? Is that my eyebrow raised?
Certainly not. It's just me looking dazed.

7

Would you prefer desire? Or call it lust?
I call it vertigo, or plain disgust.

8

Let's break up the line. Let us instead stroll
around the park and talk about your soul.

9

I prefer a motto to a top hat. I prefer
an indiscretion. Leather perhaps. Or fur.

10

I'm going to sleep. I'm off to dream the light
inside my head where it is never night.

Anxiety

Ghostlight

Early morning. Light
hesitant. Under the door
a thin strip of it

waiting to enter
the room like a ghost, stealthy,
dressed in its faint grey

shift, drifting between
times of day, as if morning
remained unsettled.

Where are we going
with ourselves? What are the hours
to be completed

before we can wake
into ourselves? Something comes
between the morning

and its conclusions.
Our eyes are half closed, awake
but unreceptive.

Are the ghosts prepared
for revelations? Will they
tell us everything?

Is any day new
to itself, unhaunted, clear
about its future?

Are the ghosts angry?
Are they settled to their fate
of mere hovering?

Something welcomes day
and all its ghosts, opens doors
and lets light stroll in.

On Getting Lost

Let's get lost.

CHET BAKER

You are looking lost
in the mirror. Are your hands
in front of your face?

There are so many
objects in the universe
of the self to lose.

Let's begin with work.
What has become of the hours
you spent doing it?

Let's say a zebra
or some exotic species
wakes you from a dream.

A tarantula
is slowly making its way
across your dream floor.

This too is your work.
These lost hours are your creatures
and must be noted.

Check your Book of Hours.
Wander through the calendar
of lost animals.

The faces they make
emerging from the mirror –
is yours among them?

You and the creatures
inhabit the same mirror.
You all come and go.

No one speaks for you.
Adjust your face and get on.
One's enough of you.

Even those faint hands
were formed in a universe
that has now vanished.

At the Train Window

Somewhere on the train
there is a face that is yours
moving past shadows.

Beyond the window
another self. Beyond it
more, and again more.

Every reflection
at every window offers
possibilities:

all one might have been
but won't be now. Such sadness
and such indifference.

It's a miracle
living with shadows, to watch
them in ghost windows.

Here is where we are,
right here, with all our faces.
Where else should we be?

Being anywhere
is good enough. Each window
and each face. Yet strange.

Beyond the ghost selves,
ghost battalions; faint hosts
in pale uniforms.

Strangest of all, this
host of shadows, this army
constantly moving.

And then to arrive
at a point on the track, found
as if never lost.

The Engine Turns

Sometime the dreaming
has to stop but meanwhile night
continues dreaming.

Out of the waking
arise the subjects of dream,
the lower levels

moving into gear,
the engine that throbs into
a conscious morning.

Under the closed lid
the eye begins to swivel
in its oiled socket.

The organs splutter
into a different rhythm,
everything pumping,

and body carries
itself forward. Time begins,
wakes to new order.

But nothing changes.
The dream with its depth charge
waits in the empty shell,

and the shell remains
husked in darkness. The window
opens to daylight

that doesn't enter
the room, that is still darkness,
still the night body.

What to do with night,
with the residue, with dream,
the body, the day?

What to do with it?
What to do with the questions?
What with the answers?

Naming and shaming

Suspicion we know,
apprehension follows us
like anxiety.

They are animals
of the household. Here's the dog
that lopes behind us,

here the small cat glimpsed
at the window, here the crows
in the high branches.

Wherever we go
they follow. Some we don't see,
like the common rat

trundling through the yard
in the dead hours, the beetle
tapping on damp wood

but we know their names
and call them to us as they
call us in return.

The names are many
but we keep inventing more,
as if the creatures

were multiplying.
Hence the apprehension, hence
the anxiety,

hence the suspicion
that all we have invented
is a catalogue

of what can't be named,
as if naming were comfort
or peace, or beauty.

The Leaves

I have sat in crowds,
and watched the figures swaying
as the wind shifted,

sitting among them
as though I didn't belong
with the leaves and clouds.

What has brought them here,
like leaves swept into rough piles?
What now divides us?

Who are these people,
these leaves, and those scuffed clouds
at their unknown rout?

Here is their autumn
and their winter, and the clouds
I watch blurting by.

Here are the bodies.
Here is the dust they fly through
given a stiff wind.

Given that stiff wind
they scuttle and disappear
even as they rise.

We have lived in crowds
and moved with the clouds. The leaves
have swirled round our feet.

We are together
and we can't help that. The seats
are vacant, leaves blown.

This is our own dust.
This is the wind in the leaves
that also shifts clouds.

Glass

The wind had stopped dead.
The clouds hovered at a loss.
The light was unchanged.

Into the vacuum
slid something unrecognised,
neither wind nor light,

but it was no new
state of affairs. Nothing changed
in our perception.

Sometimes a thin sheet
of glass is interposed. Clear,
still, immaculate,

nothing written there,
nothing of significance
in its mere presence

and nothing changes
except perhaps the presence
faintly registered,

an uneasiness
about the clouds or the light,
the lack of movement.

And this was like that,
as if history had stopped
breathing or gone blind

as it does sometimes
forget how to breathe and sees
only the stillness

which was where we were,
in the middle of such things,
or maybe the end.

Variations after Sappho

Midnight.
The moon and the
Pleiades both vanish.
Time ticks by. Here is the sofa.
Here me.

*

The moon
keeps vanishing.
Midnight, the Pleiades...
Alone with time and that damn bed
again.

*

Where are
the Pleiades?
Gone, along with the moon.
Alone in bed at midnight with
the hours.

*

It's late.
Beyond midnight.
Where has the moon vanished?
And the Pleiades? What's the time?
Who's there?

*

Always
too late. The moon
and the Pleiades gone.
Midnight. Restless. In bed again.
Alone.

*

Midnight
comes and goes. Moon
climbs and fades. Pleiades
gone for a burton but the bed
remains.

    *

Pining.
Alone. The moon
and the Pleiades lost
to midnight. Where has the time gone,
dear bed?

    *

Desire
won't let me rest.
It has eaten both moon
and Pleiades. Midnight. It's time
for bed.

    *

Alone
after midnight,
the absence of both moon
and Pleiades leaves just a bed
and lust.

    *

Time shifts
on. With moon gone
the Pleiades follow.
Soon there's just bed and me. Midnight.
Yearning.

It Never Quite Goes, the Sense of Anxiety

(for Elaine Feinstein)

It never quite goes, the sense of anxiety,
however you dress, whatever you do,
however renowned for wit or sobriety,

however established in grown-up society,
however you seem to be one of the crew,
it never quite goes, the sense of anxiety.

Where is your place in life's rich variety?
You stand in the mirror, you look through and through,
forget all your wit, forget your sobriety,

forget the big money, forget the propriety,
no point in upgrading, no point making new,
it never quite goes, the sense of anxiety.

There once was a man with a mouth full of piety,
he spoke till the words no longer rang true,
however he spiced them with wit and sobriety.

We don't want a fight, we don't want a riot, we
just want a moment of clear icy blue,
but there we are still with the sense of anxiety.

It lies far beyond us, the ultimate quiet we
hope to achieve that is never in view.
It never quite goes the sense of anxiety
for all your fine wit, for all your sobriety.

The Voices

One voice was picking itself off the floor,
another was ringing bells at the front door,
a third was shouting nonsense. There were more.

The voice of the old woman on the stairs,
the voice of Goldilocks and the Three Bears,
the voice of the man minding his own affairs.

The voice that held itself like a frail glass,
the voices on the train that we watched pass,
the breaking voice at the back of the class.

It was the night. A crowd of voices. Streets
with dogs and poor, the barks and brays and bleats,
reiterations, cries, endless repeats.

We heard the voices speaking very low,
familiar voices that we didn't know,
the voice that stuck, the voice that once let go.

Let go, the voice said. Letting go is best.
Stray lines, the overheard, the voice addressed,
and so into the night with all the rest.

The Yellow Room

1

Late father, you mystery, father of diminishing returns,
how do you weigh in the scale now, by what measure should I
examine you, when you are literally dust, which is nothing
but dust, not a meaning that might any day cohere
into the complex singularity that was addressed by name.

There should, I feel, be something solid about a name,
something gathered and whole, something that brought us here
as if by appointment, that had not arisen out of nothing
but out of name itself, the point at which you become an I
and to which the whole that is gathered eventually returns.

2

Once there was a room which was, like any other room,
fit to be born into or to stare out from, a room half-darkness,
half unquenchable light. Someone might lie down in it
or sit at a table, engaged in the act of doing and thinking,
inhabiting the room into which you as a self were born.

Let me imagine that moment, the instant of being born,
carried into a world that is not particularly thinking
of your particular moment, unconcerned with your place in it.
Time starts collapsing: it vanishes into the musty darkness
it waits in and fills up every secret corner of the room.

3

Chairs and sofas and pictures and sideboards and mornings. The door
is open. The noise of the morning is wheels, bells and cries.
The street is the one street. The house, one among many
closed universes, rushes backwards in time as you thrust forward.
You have arrived just in time, just as time was closing,

closing and collapsing, just as the door itself was closing.
There never will be another opportunity to look forward
to this. It is at this point that you become the many.
I am trying to distinguish your cry from all those other cries,
but all there is is the door, which is by now a closed door.

4

I understand nothing.

I have followed no trail.

When leaves move against the wall, it is no language.

When sun strikes the leaves it is an exclamation without sound.

I overhear it is all incompletion,   the tongues of leaves the open mouths
        of flowers.

Things happen. They stand in rows. They form orderly queues. They are
        hungry.

I cannot begin to unpick the clues without language. I need to understand
                what a clue is   what language is.

These lines are blown across the page as in a gust.

        I must order them.

5

These stanzas are closed rooms closing on themselves
with stiff internal doors. I enter, stirring a draught,
raising the corners of newspapers, and the reader
rises, or raises an eyebrow, briefly to register
an entrance, then returns to the fascinating article

he was reading, himself becoming an article
in the space provided, and I am not sure how to register
his presence, or yours, my patient, magnificent reader.
The doors of our meeting seem to permit of a draught.
Closed doors must have been opening themselves.

6

Listen, do you hear the sea? Neither can I,
except in this narrow gap as it runs under the door.
The prom is down the street, the wind is rising
like a reader disturbed in his reading. The sea
is as dark as the night, as salty as your lungs

where you stand looking out, filling your lungs
with sea air. You have some business with the sea,
this is why you slept and woke and keep rising
each morning. This is why you must open the door
to listen out for the question. Where am I? Who am I?

7

So you lie in bed, as you were, as defenceless and small
as an anecdote, a one-line perfection, and here come
the elders, the old with their gifts of sweets and cakes,
their melted offerings, and a faint yellow smell that follows
them about that is nothing to be ashamed of,

which is neither soiling nor wetting, but down to being of
a place just like this, that is yellow, from which must follow
the story the old will not tell you, where are no cakes
but a faint yellow light to which whole cities have come,
to this room, to this house, something irreducibly small.

8

Conjuring bodies out of
                thin   air as they
        appear cut and dried

it being thus and
                thus   out of thin blood
        out of the window of the room you are trapped in

listen   what do you hear
                what construction what
        peculiarity of growth

decline and
        rain that has its body
    with earth   for conjuration

take that chair, sit on it, hold still
        feel the weight
    of the rain the dimensions of the room

here is the carpet, here is the sideboard
        here is the table
    here is the window and there, the door.

9

What is certain is fear. What is plain is the silence.
Ghosts drift from the door of the yellow room
and vanish immediately, fading from memory
as they enter a train or a brickyard and the dark
hallway is empty and the river is bristling with ice.
This is the text of the hallway. This is the silence
read only behind the eyes. This is the plain room
one clings to and loses, that's hardly a memory,
more an engagement with the metaphor of dark
and the mouths of the dead glimpsed through the ice.

10

This is the street of crocodiles where the attic
is populated by misconceptions, where the full grin
of the moon in the skylight is a candle dripping
itself into a curve. The menagerie of the imagination
roosts in your bed, becomes you, dear father.

This is the room in the street where every dead father
continues living after the rituals of the imagination.
This is the room where wax disfigures night, dripping
a hot caul, where the moon is only a spectral grin
that belongs with the menagerie in the attic.

11

What if we cannot emerge from the attic? What if the bed
we sleep in is merely a stopover? What if the door opens
letting in death like a night visitor, unannounced, cold,
peremptory, uniformed, final? What if we dream ourselves
into being like this, becoming an infinitely vulnerable corpse?

This is the room and the bed inhabited by a corpse.
This is a photograph captioned 'Merely ourselves'.
These are the windows that are letting in the cold.
What happens then when the window is wide open?
What happens then with the corpse alive in the bed?

12

can we tell the fantastical from the real
        I doubt it, except by gazing at the fresh
                snow and considering look hands
    as a metaphor

        and for what? there's the shape
    and there's what it means and the cold
                is only a partial meaning and the light
                only a partial light
shall we try to unravel it, retrace our poor
                steps back to their source
        the locus of their floating before you in the snow

which is metaphor but real to the missing birds
            who do not visit which is death to them
                    driven snow

    but who is doing the driving, father, do you see
            do you see how this metaphor works
        what it does and why it does it

because I don't, dear father, I'm guessing
    as always, guessing at the cold and the feel
                    of the snow in which something
            is it you? is buried, your hands
        with their fingers of ice as metaphor

13

When I imagine you as a boy I see myself
resembling a self that is you. We're alike
in the room of our history, that clouded sky
we glimpse through the windows of rooms
that are similar, all being temporary shelters

in which the imagination occasionally shelters
with her sister, anxiety, sharing double rooms
in a hotel with its offers of everything under the sky,
that is always and everywhere essentially alike
in whose mirrors I have sometimes glimpsed myself.

14

You have parked in the street and arrive at the front door.
You turn the key, enter the hallway and take off your hat.
Outside it is still a world of hats and quiet suits
under quiet overcoats. Your tie too is quiet.
It is as if the fear of disturbing the world were too much

to be coping with, that being a terrifying too-much
at the heart of things. So it is best to be quiet.
Quiet between the wars. Quiet in offices. Suits
cut from similar cloths. The felt of your hat
over your face, your mouth like a half-closed door.

15

There is no history that is not secret history.
There is no breathing that is not public breathing.
You are a sentient being, that fabulous zero
the planet keeps producing. You are nature on the run.
You are the glitch in everything official.

I name you so in order to be official,
to have you outed in the records. I will run
a tight ship. Look here is my signature: *Zero*.
I am the Captain Nemo of the craft, the breathing
tenant of what I officially designate as history.

16

Consider the soul
     as a small room with a key and
   a window partially open if only so we can breathe.
The crowds in the street is ourselves,
        our fellow conspirators against the the conspirators

        You watch a man at a task you note
  the concentration as he floats into it you watch
   a woman in an office under the fluorescent sun
      of her daytime as it darkens towards
          evening

    and it's all floating off   the fierce knot
  in the nerves   the whiplash behind the brow   the light

blowing

    through the streets and into the houses
the rooms–chairs–stools–tables–settees–beds
      the sad furniture of the universe

the birthright.

17

Always in the room, never setting forth
into the street, down to the dock and on
to the waiting ship, which is waiting on you.
Here we are, here's the jetty, the water
slurping and swelling with its vast hunger.

It may be that the room is filled with hunger.
It may be that your glass is full of water.
It may that out there is only a you
waiting to be filled. And so you step on
to the ship that is for ever setting forth.

18

Here is a place that has been filed down
into the finest particulars and you tell me
it is anywhere and I answer that's true
but insist on the domain of the unexceptional
which is its own special place, precise and perfect.

Not that any particular place is perfect.
You too, my father, are unexceptional.
We're not anyone's chosen, we are not the true
residual trace of any God that says *Me*.
Listen, dad, I am getting the truth down.

Disaster Zone: Flood

Event

Now it's getting late
the body's weight increases
with the weight of hours.

Weight of the body,
of being, of dead spaces
in the mind and heart.

Each day adds its own
freight of hours, its fat purse
carefully emptied.

So an afternoon
raises itself and expands
its enormous chest.

And the rain begins
its delicate late concert
of spindly fingers.

The tremendous trees
buck like horses and the light
outside is in them.

The leaves shudder
and indulge themselves in flight.
The wind goes flying.

Even the small stream
seems determined to buckle
and scurry away.

What might we not do,
what might we not aspire to
if we were water?

Events weigh with us.
Hence the curtains, the desk light,
entrance and evening.

Enter our blood stream,
tree, wind, river, rain, window.
Lighten our bodies.

Surge

As the wind dies down
the sea picks up. So land falls
and water rises.

And the brittle shore
breaks, much as the sea can break,
constantly broken.

We are disasters
on the edge of our own shores,
dreaming and woken.

Nothing permanent
about us. If sea can break
so can shore and cliff.

The thought of the sea
is a form of rising. Sky
over high water.

The church with its hymns.
The sailors with their shanties.
Sand with its shifting.

In every cadence
the certainty of water,
the howling of wind.

The tide closing in
on the throat. The billowing.
The wretched dark cloud.

We dream beginnings
and endings. Everything moves
to its own cadence.

The long run is now.
The sea constantly rolling
into the present.

Listening to the weather

Suddenly words poured
out of drains into gardens
too drenched to hear them.

Trees and bushes were
listening to the *ursprache*
of rising thunder.

The lake strained to hear
the utterances of light
spreading over it.

The world was all ears,
the fields preparing their notes
for a bright future.

But when the wind spoke
loud and clear to a tumult
of rain, the rain heard.

And when the fields spoke
water and the sky bellowed
air, it was meaning.

People were measuring
the tides, calibrating loss
by the yard and mile.

There were the data
properly laid out and crunched
into neat pie-charts.

Language was effort.
The sky could say what it liked
with its dark grammar

of gesture and shift.
We were at cross-purposes
and longing for sun.

Umbrella

Things that speak to you
have no home. They just arrive
as if passing through.

Yesterday nothing.
The day before it, nothing.
Nothing is normal.

The great storms. The winds
that blow a whole street away
were nothing before.

Then there you are, wet,
struggling against the fury
of things beyond you.

I watch a woman
back into the gale, her lost
umbrella spinning.

For a split second
she wonders if she should chase
after it, then shrugs

and faces the wind
as she must. Look there! a house
detached and floating.

Suffering begins
elsewhere. Yesterday nothing.
It's the way of things.

Things that speak to you
arrive and are gone. They leave
their passing behind.

Here they are, in you.
They have no home. They must lodge
where they can. And do.

But

Something in the mind
had changed direction. It ran
backwards like the street

he had just dreamt. Time
meant nothing here. It was space
by another name,

an air to walk through.
Perhaps it was death. Perhaps
it was just shadow,

but what was unwrapped
was too bright for death. Shadow
was what it produced.

There was the sea, bright
as a tin tray in sunlight,
dimpled, glittering.

And this was the street
with the sea at the far end.
This was the clear light.

It was the waking
everyone wakes to, in light
without time, in space,

in a universe
all dimension, no clock,
all sea and no shore.

These are interim
solutions, he said, just notes
on the road to sleep.

But sleep had vanished
up its own sleeve. No answer
there but street and sea.

Wreckage

Go to the wreckage,
the ruins under the house.
You will recognise

the rooms you once knew
by their dimensions. It is
the familiar

that eludes you. Go
through them all, one by one. Go
to the tightest space

and note the dizzy
height of the ceiling. What's wrong
with you? It's your house.

But no, it's never
like that. The recognition
is false. There's nothing

to know here. Only
the space made by memory
in alien fabric

which can look like this
or that, as can those you know,
as you can yourself.

And out in the street
the wrecked persist in wearing
the same haunted look

of recognition.
This is your parallel life,
your sheets of paper,

your pens and pencils,
the food left on the table
you must eat or die.

A Dream of New Washing

The wind that tumbled
fences and upended trees
has been forgotten.

There is no loud noise
in the head. We hear nothing
to trouble our dreams.

Something is relieved
of the task of recalling.
Make me new, it sings.

So we make it new
and remark how an ill wind
has blown itself out.

Look at the washing,
we say, see how still it is,
sheets hanging straight down:

the past drips from it;
the wind no longer ruffles
clean shirt-sleeves and soon

we will bring them in,
iron them and replace them
in cool dark cupboards.

Now all shall be well
as was promised, and will be
promised every time.

The new washing moves
in a delicate new way,
nudged by a new wind.

An hour of sunlight
fills an old room. One white cloud
makes a whole weather.

The Mathematics of Freedom
(for Denis Gabor)

Hologram

Now I am nowhere, neither here nor there
so what you see before you is another.
I am a compound something. Nothing there
of what I was, though once there was a there
to belong to that was no illusion.
Walk round me. Now you see me? I'm just there
within the glass that is itself not there
as place or thing, purely as an image.
This is life as you see it. This is my image
faintly glowing. I seem to have been there
as if for ever, and you can walk right round me
as though that non-object in space were me.

We're nowhere half the time. If this were me
talking to you, you'd know that I was there
yet different, with another name for me.
We change locations. You are bound to find me
as elusive as I do, as would another.
I'm the beam in your eye. That child was me
at home. The man you're talking to is me
as an illusion. Reality is illusion,
nor is this real. Appearance is illusion.
I am the scientist of what is there
but goes on missing. I am the wind's image
in a window. I am light's own image.

But look, the world may be perceived as image
and yet have laws that apply to you and me.
I profess myself. I am simply the image
that I see, my own self being the image
here photographed. My parents who were there
combed my hair and tidied me. My image

was what they made it. I was the very image
of them. Although a child I was another,
an image in a mirror that is itself another.
I was diffracted, refracted. I became an image
in the mirror, the mirror that was illusion.
Everything in the mirror was illusion.

Realities of furniture, clothes: illusion.
We are spectacle. My numbers are the image
of real forces that work over illusion.
Life's engineered beyond the faint illusion
of appearance. The man in the coat is me.
The man talking to you now is no illusion.
This is the hologram of my voice. Illusion
returns to haunt us both because you're there
beside me in the mirror that is there
before you at a time that's no illusion.
My body is a power that may be other.
My heart and mind persist as that another.

Born this or that, we enter one another
through space and try the senses as illusion.
What is this voice within the being another?
Is it produced by mind? Is mind another,
a form of vision? We die to become an image.
I am, like you, trapped in something other,
an appearance mooted only as another.
My voice too moves, it is the trace of me
in the silence of an image that's beyond me.
Turn on the laser beam. Lend me another
moment. Now let our two images meet there.
Enter this moment. Just for a moment be there.

The sense of being neither here nor there,
of no importance, not being a me,
is one we claim serves only as an image.
Darling, enter with me this real illusion,
become spectacle and remain another.

The Definition of Liberty

What Abraham Lincoln said ninety years ago is still true, 'the world has never had a good definition of the word liberty'

DENIS AND ANDRÉ GABOR, *The Concept of Statistical Freedom and Its Application to Social Mobility*

You see that man teetering down the alleyway
in the rain without a coat? I'd call him free.
Freedom is this. The river as it trundles
past the buildings. It is the mouth that moves
and speaks. It is the overflow that proves
the current. Liberty is the burning candles
on my table, my pulse, and the rule of three.
It is any day of the week except Sunday.

How to formulate this? How to describe
the limits that define us? Let me take
this orange from the bowl. Let me imagine
night before night's due. Let me write down
your number. Let the monarch assume the crown.
Let the mother of god remain a virgin.
The laws are beautiful of which we make
assumption, an us that we may circumscribe.

Circumscription is the best that we can do. Feel
the hand of that thin child. Count up his bones.
We have a regular shape a mirror can reflect.
Are you twice as happy as you were before?
Is the child ill? Is the child's family poor?
Consider the frail wings of this small insect.
Consider the wind. Listen to the groans
of the house as it bears its load. Summon the real.

And so he struggled out of his own skin.
We try so hard to be. He was intelligent
and hungry. He observed the rotten politics
of dying. He could count them on his teeth.
This is the freedom we want. This is the wreath
on the coffin. This is our mathematics.
This, surely, is what the experiments meant.
Here is the rain. Here is your coat. Come in.

Small Change

> But if we come to the community as a whole, new problems arise, because prices do not then remain the same if output changes as a result of a shift in taste. One way to deal with it is to curve the money surface
>
> 'Pro Memoria, Theory of Freedom'. Letter to André Gabor

He curved the palm of his hand as to receive
the blessing that was our small change.
The result, a moment's release: small change.

Beef

I may generally prefer chicken to beef, but after several months on
chicken only, I must have some beef for a change – otherwise I would
drop to a lower level of satisfaction. It seems that herein lies one of
the most important aspects of the freedom concept: man is generally
happier if he can vary his consumption pattern. It is of course possible
to swamp this effect simply by considering periods which are long
enough for each actually exercised choice to occur at least once,
– say by taking the year as the unit and describing the consumption
 pattern as 300 helpings of chicken and 64 helpings of beef.

'Pro Memoria, Theory of Freedom'. Letter to André Gabor

Butter mountains! Wine lakes! Mass graves of beef!
The genocide of chickens! The destruction of the grasses
over a single lifetime. And let us not forget the Continents of Grief
on which the poor live in their various subclasses.

Inside each freedom, another freedom. Inside each sun
another sun still vaster, still hotter, too vast to calculate,
the sky at liberty to collapse, the world to come undone
and all the freedoms waiting for far too long, arriving late.

Nutritional Value

> Until objective measures of nutritional value were introduced, there was
> no common basis on which diets could be judged, and until the measurable
> aspect of heat VMs discovered, it could be decided by majority vote only
> whether a room was hot or cold.
>
> DENIS AND ANDRÉ GABOR, *The Concept of Statistical Freedom
> and Its Application to Social Mobility*

Behold the economy. Behold its tolerable limits.
You have a certain liberty of movement within it.
If I were younger I would have a variety of choices.
If I were the crowd in the street I would have several voices.

You have your part of the pavement, I have mine.
It doesn't take a theory of, let us call it, intelligent design
to allow each of us a flagstone in the whole,
to postulate a value for, let us call it, the soul.

I close this brief lecture by citing several sources.
Why take an old car when you have a field of horses?
Why stop at zero, why at one, when you have so many?
And now I am free to answer questions, if there are any.

Eternity

If we say that the hour spent in the dentist's waiting room seemed
like eternity, we acknowledge both an acceptance of the objective
measure of time and its inability to take account of accompanying
circumstances.

DENIS AND ANDRÉ GABOR, *The Concept of Statistical Freedom
and Its Application to Social Mobility*

It was the freedom to unmake she desired.
She would unmake herself and start again
knowing what was to come. She would walk
along the street knowing what awaited her.

She walked in her own beautiful space. She spoke
in the voice that had grown in her delicate throat
like a flower that issued at her lips before
words assumed meaning and the space crumpled.

Her face was ageing. She was either putting on
or losing weight. Her eyes were growing larger.
How much space they occupied! How much space
there was to be part of! She could feel her body

moving forward into time as down a street
to the future she was longing not to meet.

The Instruments

Since we have grown up with accepted objective measures of time, distance, heat, weight, pressure, etc., we see little point in blaming the instruments if their evidence departs from our subjective impressions, and rather say that our senses deceived us.

DENIS AND ANDRÉ GABOR, *The Concept of Statistical Freedom and Its Application to Social Mobility*

1

If we could only calculate in degrees
or by some splendid rococo equation
in which the givens cannot be taken away.

We have hours, minutes, seconds, and our lives.
We are aware that we miscalculated.
We made choices. We might have chosen better.

Confessions! Abstractions! Is there nothing better
than the sum of these two hands, the calculated
movement of hands moving through our lives?

I can count minutes as time flows away.
I can subtract an hour's listless equation,
Hands move through space in minutes and degrees.

2

She was taking my temperature. Her hand
lay on my brow. I was almost three,
and lucky, statistically, to be alive.

A degree or two of difference is all it takes.
A minute or two earlier or later.
At any moment your number can come up.

I sat beside you. You were waking up
I had been there for hours. It was much later
than I imagined. People had made mistakes.

I was tired out by then, more dead than alive.
I looked at my watch again. It was past three
in the morning. Late now too. Give me your hand.

3

He tried the violin. It was expensive
but hollow in sound. It lacked resonance,
that rich belly of sound. It could not sigh
as though it were merely counting out the bars
and waiting for God to arrive When God comes
he enters through the ear and sighs like music.

My neck is slender, my belly full. My music
is my body as it is. Nobody comes
to me pretending to be divine. My bars

are locked. A millimetre, one faint sigh
of wind in a forest is my resonance.
Language is cheap. It's freedom that's expensive.

Hologram as Light

Already he was far too real. The image produced
by the process was the shadow of an answer.
He left his home before the killing started.

His mathematics lay beyond the borders. He fell
into a language that was not yet style but growing.
Meanwhile the numbers remained strictly numbers.

How to become another? How to solve a problem
that is capable of solution? How to produce a figure
that might be balanced on the flesh and on the nerves?

Everything was always far too real for comfort.
The future was waiting in the queue, his and others'
and the line was stretching deep into the moment.

To engineer the world! To render it operative!
To turn the ingenious into the consoling!
There was truth enough out there to put a sum to.

Meanwhile the sky grows inky. Meanwhile the weeping
rain, the thunder under the skin, the equation of death
as known. Meanwhile the world, its image and its light.

Disaster Zone: The Missing

Disaster Zone

For no known reason
it happened, as if reason
were not important,

because no reason
is never reason enough.
So when it happened

and the sky behaved
in an irrational way
they could not see it,

not through the dense cloud,
not through the cover of night
nor through the moment.

Because a moment
is never just a moment
but a consequence

that is perfection,
that is a brilliant sky
full of clarities

that are solutions.
These are our perfect bodies
holding together

according to rules
of flesh and bone and reason,
they said and believed

while in their bodies
the reasons of disaster
worked their own reason.

A Low Flying Plane

Somewhere in a sky
purring with cloud and light, planes
talk to each other.

What is the language
at the bottom of the throat,
that deep-lying growl?

When does it enter
the hangar of the stomach,
how does it park there?

From nowhere at all
the planes appear. The sky cracks
under them and bursts.

I'm trying to hear
the subtext of this, the blown
language of such noise,

the sense of low flight,
the way it presses dense air
into liquid shape.

Then the plane is gone
but things have changed. The tongue,
the ear, the dead sound.

Runway

Wisps, strings, ribbons, lace,
capillaries, filaments,
delicate networks...

something sustains us
in tension. Hunting for it
among images,

unsustainable
and incomprehensible,
there remain only

wisps, threads and the rest,
a brilliant shimmering
under closing eyes,

still more images,
and then this: an aeroplane
solid as the earth

and a faint signal
among the neural networks
of the universe,

a twitch of terror,
a sudden disappearance,
a broken fibre

as if it could burst
from the skull in mid flight, land,
plant its full cargo

on the frail runway
of the imagination
weighted with absence.

It is the absence
together with the runway.
It is the cargo.

The Missing

Where are the missing,
we ask and, look, here they are
inside the pages.

Others hold pages.
They don't seem to be missing.
They're standing right there.

How many of us
have vanished leaving a face
or a description?

Say it is raining
and people are in a rush
and don't want to stop.

Say shops are closing
the faces folded away.
and the missing lost

in their own version
of elsewhere where another
rain is falling, soft

as the growing dark
of which we become a part
treading as softly.

We have left footsteps
but have hardly touched the ground
in our passage through.

We have sold the pass
along with the soaked papers.
We have sold ourselves.

Here are the missing.
We count ourselves among them.
We hold our papers.

Lament

Sometimes you see it
huddled in a tight corner
of the closing eye.

It is not a plea
but a statement. The eyes stop
speaking once they've closed.

Something has gone out,
something has haunted itself
into vanishing.

We have a grammar
for this kind of thing. We read
the future backwards

into the present
as it rushes towards us
at menacing speed.

There it is again,
your death looking back at you
smaller than ever,

its vanishing point
lodged in someone else's eye
just as it closes.

One moment too far
is already a lifetime.
There's nothing in it.

Now the eyes have closed
the statement remains unfixed
hanging in the air.

All punctuation
is ending. Every closed eye
finishes a sentence.

Singular

All our singular
voices were joined in the choir
of the vanishing.

We were not ourselves.
We were a single body
and so we vanished.

It was a single
terror, indivisible.
We could not know it.

Out there the planets
were counting themselves. Their eyes
were looking away.

The terror out there
was happening inside us
individually.

We had dreamt it all
before. It was quite common.
It was what joined us.

We were united
in our singularity,
our dreams and dying.

We dream all the time
of this commonality,
the wild singular.

So when the water
rose and the wind gathered
we knew it as dream.

The wind was wailing
with us. I too was wailing
with others as choir.

We can't grieve ourselves.
The water and wind will have
to do it for us.

Backspace

1

Whatever frozen
piece of clear sky goes missing
vanishes like us.

2

Simply to vanish
is intolerable. Sky
does not quite vanish.

3

Any erasure
is a denial. Blank sky
does not deny us.

4

We can't comprehend
our vanishing universe,
our compact with time.

5

To have been erased
from history is to have
been detached from time.

6

Something deletes us,
presses the backspace. We fall
out of existence.

7

It is an offence
to memory. It is death
without a death list.

8

Let us at least see
the list from which our names
have been deleted.

9

Let us read ourselves
out of the sky as by right.
We did once matter.

10

Because we mattered,
didn't we? We are matter.
We can't have vanished.

Cargo

Consider the drowned
packing the sea and rising
like a dank mountain.

Crowding the water,
packed close like cargo, the drowned
vanish unlisted.

How deep the sea is,
how fierce and cold, untroubled
by its history.

We have history
in which we drown our sorrows
as in saltwater.

We don't understand
death in the way the sea does.
We set out in hope.

Now we lie, piled up,
as if we were intended
to be together.

But nothing is meant.
The sea does not bear meaning.
It is just a throat.

We too have our throats
but they are filled with water
and grief and money.

Those who ferry us
betray us. We can't trust them
but rely on them.

You will recall us
in your private drowned moments.
You will recall us.

The Books

The books are restless.
They are in wintery mood,
their voices urgent.

What the books whisper
is what we would not mention
in conversation.

They know more. Guess more.
They have been where we can't go
in the clothes we wear.

They are unsettled
when we would be still. They hear
what we cannot hear.

We open a page
and fall into its cold depths
to sink like a stone.

We talk in clichés
they despise. They don't like us.
They will shake us off.

Too many voices
to register. Too many
lost conversations.

They hover in time
like bad omens. They flap wings,
their frantic pages

cloud the sky over.
They precipitate. They rain
down on us. They soar.

They are the darkness
in our bones that continue
to glow like dead fires.

Stillness

1

An old man in white t-shirt and denim shorts in the café of the bazaar
   so thin he is barely there, his hair too thin, sits immobile at the
   metal table. He is so still I think he is meditating but when I
   look harder he seems to be taking his left pulse with his right
   hand. Then he takes his right pulse with his left hand. Each
   time a couple of minutes of absolute stillness. Then he folds his
   hands, palm upward as if to catch something from heaven. Judging
   from his expression he looks to be in despair but maybe that is
   just his way of keeping still. Maybe this is the heart of stillness,
   the capturing of it in moment after moment, capturing it with a
   purpose but little hope, like rain between dry spells or a moment
   of dryness between the rains.

2

Beggars too are models of stillness. This one has bent himself so out
   of shape he looks permanent. His knee is higher than his shoulder,
   one leg ends in a stump and is tucked under the other but
   somehow off the ground. He is like a puzzle that one or other
   god has tried to solve but gave up, walked off and forgot or left
   to another god to sort out. His gaze is fixed on the ground or
   maybe it is the ground that has mesmerised him so it is not
   within his willpower to raise his eyes. In any case it is stalemate:
   zugzwang. The stillness is itself forgotten. It is like those pointless
   pennies in his glass begging jar in which light is the only thing
   that moves.

Ice Cap

And the earth was ice. The high-rise settlements were
strictly nineteenth century, as if we could be here and there
at once, frosted into chilling miraculous air.

Our breath was magic, palaces froze about us.
The sunlight played beneath a skin of ice.
We desired the cold. We wanted the the great white dress

of snow to gather into pleats, to cut air into slices.
We were calendar and circle and the seasons. Our faces
were blue, perfect seas with icebergs for noses.

Bring us round. Breathe on us. Perfect our absolute zero.
Wheel round the rusty universe in your barrow
and let us bury our heads in it like a frozen arrow.

Maghreb

Look, there are pearls of rain that hang and drip
in the grey light. There's the high wall with its fists
of flint, and the leaves with their green palms
open to the sky, till a gust exposes their delicate wrists

and they shudder and lift and the grey light remains.
And this is what's strange, this being anywhere
with a familiar incomprehensibility, the birds
familiar to the sky, relaxed in its homely air,

yet mad and otherwise, strange even to themselves.
You sit at your table, friend, at home with the curious
paraphernalia of your body as I am with mine.
I feel our peculiar, polyvalent, unutterably various

languages shifting underfoot. To me the names
I pass between my lips – Algiers, Tunis, Rabat –
are as fresh clothes in which my body is renewed.
May your fresh clothes be mine. May the desert

at your feet burn mine.

The Hotel Opens

Chord and Ornament

The architecture
of music: concrete, steel, glass,
wood, the dizzy heights.

Sometimes bones mutter
under flesh. Winter singing
through hair, fingernails.

What saws through the bones
like that? What is it that music
destroys and rebuilds?

Music and blood. Rain
in the valley of the bones.
The pulse in the wrist.

The fingers moving
as to a score in blank air:
the wind forms the hand.

Nothing in your hands,
except, when you open them,
the music flies out.

That scoop of shadow
flying across the lit floor:
chord and ornament.

The ghost of Schubert
enters. The house is shaking.
It will pass. It does.

Voices underground:
music tapping its way out
of death and thunder.

When the last trumpet
dies away the brief silence
germinates, draws breath.

A Flowering

The hotel opens
like a flower. No, it bursts
into the air, wild

as the notional
wind driving it into life,
al fresco, fountain

of column and pier
in an architectural
garden of graces.

It craves the sky, holds
itself in check, as by root
and stem, then explodes

as anything might
when moving between two forms,
that which is defined

and that which begins
without a definition
but seeks firm essence.

Here is the windflower
that discovers itself in
its own flowering.

It's falling apart.
It's just holding together.
It is barely there.

When we wake the light
will look straight through us. Our eyes
will note the strangeness

of the naked light,
our pleasure in the burst flower
as it blows open.

South

Roses from the South,
the waltzes, the thunderous
galloping polkas…

Like the hand you place
on mine or the words you
speak into a locked room

they are memory
feeding on its own product,
its own betrayal.

Waltzes betray us.
Polkas run away with us.
The loud symphonies

you wept to and praised,
they are unaccountable,
no longer music

but the other side
of time behind a closed door,
something heard through walls,

the notional sound,
of imagined brilliance,
pure manner and light.

They leave us behind.
The galloping horses locked
into their breathing

simply mist the glass
through which we see and hear them.
The grand entrances

are blocked by rubble
and nostalgia. The south wind
blows on, just music.

A Quartet from Finland

What is the music
weaving the night together
like a small spider?

It wriggles this way
and that so delicately,
scuttling up and down,

you would think it had
an agenda, some design
beyond construction

transcending hunger,
when all it looks to achieve
is to build a web

and then shimmy up
and down it and to sit there
at its frail centre.

Erik Tulindberg,
you slender eight-legged slip
of a dead spider,

spinning through the night
in whatever Finland then
existed to spin in,

are you still spinning
your death on a short silk thread,
the draught still blowing

where it hangs and sways
while I wake from my own web
spun out of nowhere?

Is this my morning
or your night? Is it the two
we're both stuck between?

A Note on Photographs

The old photographs
won't stop still in their stillness.
Either they've moved on

or we have. They stare
at time, constantly surprised
by how still it is,

as we are surprised
by how fast it moves, then stops,
just as they once did,

and so, between us,
a sharp intake of breath holds
the moment, breathless

as they are, as we
will be, as though we had lost
something important

that we will not miss,
just as we will not be missed
by the vacated

moment, the meaning
of which hovers before us,
not quite as image,

but becoming one
for an instant, one as packed
as the photograph

before us, which is
older than we knew, less void,
and somehow better

than we expected,
more round, more mobile, more us,
more just everything.

Rembrandt

It was the screwed-up paper handkerchiefs
on top of the wardrobe, so much like frail skin,
dried-out, yet delicate. It was the low relief

of bags under the eyes, the tear caught in
the eye's corner. You have to crawl inside
your body in the morning. You have to grin

at the hollow reflection that seems to divide
your face in two. It is the peculiar dullness
you discern that wasn't there. However wide

you open your eyes the leaden light, the press
of death's strong finger, blurs the thing you were.
Here you are wearing that uncomfortable dress,

the vicious ruff scratching your chin, the fur
that no longer keeps you warm. The sheer discomfort!
Days collapse into days and, when you stir

gravity drags you back. Life is too short
for this, nights too long for the moon to climb.
And all that velvet! All the dark report

of endless waiting. How considerate of time
to wrap you up like this. How dense the gold
of the lightbulb declining from its prime.

You are becoming precious, your face scrolled
into a document. Let him paint you like this.
Let him caress the canvas with his terminal cold.

Blow your nose. Offer your cheek for his kiss.

Bright Room

Whether they were arms
or sticks it was hard to say
the way they lay there.

Sometimes arms are sticks
as near as makes no difference
just looking at them.

What is it to be
alive and to have such arms
as these poor bare sticks

and the room alive
with sunlight and white flowers
and the lawn outside

as if things could be
both born and dying at once
in the same bright room?

And then she opened
her eyes. She blinked and stared
about the bright room.

Should death have such arms
it would not surprise the eyes.
Eyes are what death lacks.

Open eyes are life.
When they look at death they close
for a lost moment

and the arms settle
like sticks of wood on a log
you might use for fire.

For now they were arms
and unsettled, the eyes wide
with light and flowers.

Nothing

Remains the question
of nothing, wanting nothing,
believing nothing,

thinking of nothing
but the thought of nothing, gone,
blown into thin air,

what once was body
or speech or thought or desire
of body, of self.

Remember nothing,
anticipate nothing. Dream
of nothing. Just sleep.

Assuringly blank,
the empty window, the door
that is left ajar,

the unfinished book
the untouched glass of water,
the leaving of things.

There remain the words
saying this, the sentences
formed round a space,

that build themselves room
to diminish in. Winter.
The remembered sky

growing blanker. White
spaces on blank white paper.
Does nothing have hands?

Do hands look like this?
Is there nothing we can do?
No hands? No soft feet?

Room with a View

There was no going
or returning. The window
was closed, the door locked.

There were the cobwebs.
There was the forgotten chair,
the empty cupboard.

Strongroom of the heart.
Is it the locked silent place
with its furniture?

Stand at the window
and look out. What do you see?
A yard. A garden.

An exterior
bathed in early morning light,
conjectural breeze.

Movement of the air,
an imagined light, a faint
stirring of red leaves.

One imagines rooms
and gardens, fills empty yards
with desire for light.

The view from the room
is also the room. Outside
a form of inside.

The forgotten chair,
the cupboard with its stale breath,
the brief dimensions

are home not hotel.
What the eye sees is comfort.
The heart in its place,

the desires in check,
the garden, the yard, the room,
all accounted for.

There's no need for keys
or a brick to break the glass.
Conjecture will do.

Filming Death

Outside – in the grounds
of the institution – birds
strut across the lawn.

There is a fountain
and benches, shaded tables,
an ample car park.

What could be better
than dying on location
as on a film set?

It's how we picture
success: comfort in old age,
summer, high cloud, sun.

Briefly cars arrive
and stop before the entrance,
leave within the hour.

Everything is brief
and yet eternal. Windows
give on to brief light.

Each breath is its own
clock. Each finger its own space.
Each name its label.

Each nagging odour
has its proper cause, The doors
open to fresh air.

Might we fall asleep
considering this? Or wake
to its permanence?

Begin the filming.
Turn on that working fountain.
Sit down. Name the birds.

Mourning: a sketch

In the end we come
to places like this: vanished
parks, demolished streets,

desperate sinkholes
of the spirit, subsidence
that can shift a house.

Drawing the city
is like conjuring thunder
from a mess of cloud,

but in the morning
the layout makes sense again
and we are somewhere.

The stranger waiting
at the unwelcoming port
narrows his bright eyes.

The traveller lost
in the great underground
leans against a wall.

The children standing
at the bus stop seek their home
on an undrawn map.

There are maps to walk
and lose ourselves in, even
without a compass

Let city and park
be at the appointed place.
Let the ground hold firm.

The Matrix Reloaded

When we dream of death
    it is of the beauty
of dealing it.

When we dream of death
    it is not ourselves
that are feeling it.

We fly between death, between
    its gaunt columns,
through the architecture

of dying, swift,
    at bullet speed,
the frozen picture

of a dance that
    continues moving
to its track

of silences, till finally
    the deafening boom
where we crack

and reform into
    ourselves for ever,
 splitting then fused,

our programmes still running
    still dealing death,
not even bruised,

just waiting to choose
    the moment of
vanishing, to appear

as ready for ourselves as stars
    are for distance,
so brilliant, so near.

Forked Tongues

Caedmon

My mouth was empty
when the words flew out, light, free,
loud, unencumbered.

I watched them swooping
over rooftops, their flight path
dazzling and certain.

They were beautiful!
How marvellous to master
the air and let go!

They made shapes in voice
and light. They were the language
of grace in movement.

Being so dazzled
I forgot everything else.
I was blank, weightless.

I became language,
a hot mouth, a form of flight
powered by rapture.

I could be written
out of the world, be nothing
but the cry of birds.

My mouth was empty,
there was nothing left in there
except a hot tongue.

Fly home dear words. Nest
in my mouth. My tongue is hot
with yearning for you.

Let me believe you.
Speak me into being. Sing
the heart of the house.

Polyphonic

While he was talking
another voice crept under
his tongue and stayed there.

The voice was not strange.
It felt quite comfortable
tucked into his mouth.

It curled there and spoke
as a shadow might when there
is room for shadows.

Nothing that is mine
can be strange, he told himself.
This too is my voice.

Reassuring words.
But the voice in his mouth sang
to a different score.

It's polyphony,
he argued but the guest voice
carried on singing:

There are things we say
that say themselves in the way
they have to be said.

Regard the flowers
nodding in the garden, lost
in their own music.

He would have listened
out of courtesy and held
his unruly tongue

but his mouth was full
of compelling flowers of speech
so he kept talking.

A Close Run Thing with the Police

Where have you put it,
the dark I mean, she asks me,
but I cannot say.

The dark's a cliché,
I plead without conviction.
There are words and states.

That's just clever talk,
though not altogether false,
and it burns my mouth.

Then I remember
those pockets filled with darkness
I had to empty.

Turn out your pockets,
says the policeman. *That dark,*
is it yours, he asks.

How did it get there?
The policeman takes a look
and shrugs. *It's legal,*

nothing important.
The drug in your possession
is your own business.

Thank you, officer.
I pocket my slip of dark
and go on my way.

That's the dark I mean,
she says. *It is your cliché.*
It's yours. It's legal.

Leave It to Us

We are moving on.
It is night. Our legs are tired
of walking through fields.

Thinking exhausts us
and feeling is a lost cause.
Time is against us.

Once we had bodies,
now there are these heavy limbs
we have to carry.

Leave them behind now:
body and mind, the grudges
you are still nursing.

Before you arrived
there was something else. The land
preceded your eyes.

All that open air
has settled into your lungs
and demands a home.

Move away from it.
There is little left for you
except words like these.

And words too must go
back to the fields they came from
to be replanted.

You must plant yourself.
You must release earth and seed.
Leave it to the wind.

Leave it to us.

Good Dog Voice

Despite the voices
there is ever more babble
and still more on hold.

Everyone's talking.
The trees are at it, the grass,
all raise their voices.

How do you speak, voice?
Will you not join the babble?
Can't you hear yourself?

I hear you all right:
rough, inarticulate,
practically howling.

Is it you speaking
for me? Someone must own you.
Come here voice. Good dog.

Don't I feed you well,
dog voice? Is your dear master
ever unfaithful?

Let's go for a walk.
I will let you off the leash
once people have gone.

There's just you and I
and those phantasmal voices
we all hear sometimes.

I'm making my home
with them in an underworld
of dogs and voices.

Lie down beside me,
dog. Let us be company
for each other, voice.

Who Crouches...

Who crouches in the aisles
Who moves owl-bruised skyward
Who cruises through nave and air
Billowing between clerestory and triforium

Who hugs hard stone or follows
The spiral stair by Caen Stone
Into treasury and spyhole
To a level, hanging O

Tritina

Every morning they waited for the postman.
They talked and fretted, or would go for a walk,
examine their nails or fetch something from the cupboard.

Even when there was nothing in the cupboard
it filled the time between rising and the postman
whose steps they listened for, recognising his walk

on the gravel drive. There was nothing but the postman.
There was always the waiting, and the long walk
up the hill. There was always the talking and the cupboard,

as if the postman could walk straight through the cupboard.

A Small Book of Melancholy

There are certain kinds of melancholy
that lend themselves like library books
as if to say, borrow me, I look like this.

I am resolved into an image you recognise
in a mirror before a face but turned away
like a pair of legs, like a body laid out.

I am an unmade bed, you say, or a wall
that needs painting. I am desolate,
plugged into bad wiring, a distant blur.

I am the ghost on the stairs, a ceiling rose
with no light fitting. I am Eggleston boiled
and discarded. I speak no particular time.

All these things offer a resolution.
Your spirit stands a few feet away from you
and demands a room of its own, with pay.

Does melancholy have the kind of anatomy
laid out in baroque English? Lend me your ear
so I may pour my condition into it.

Consider the state of the world. It does not
resolve into an image such as melancholy.
Consider the deaths, the massacres.

I cultivate suffering as an image of disgrace.
The disgraceful are running the show
and this is what they present me with.

Look through the night window. Is it open?
Is the mist drifting in any kind of answer?
Is what we borrow returnable at all?

I am such fragments. I don't seek completion
in images. I have borrowed enough light
to last me for ever in this tiny book.

A Hungarian Folk Song

A little wee bird has lately come as guest
To my garden, to my garden, and has set to build a nest
But my sorrows are so heavy they block out half the sun
And the little bird stops building, its nest half done.

Sweet little singer, bearer of my grief,
Chatter on, chatter on and bring me some relief.
Leave my heart to struggle with the dark tents of night
Warble me your pleasure, bring my soul to light.

A Photograph

Should someone ask me what life is, I'd say
this is, knowing it is only you, but reading
your face, the light enveloping it, into all faces,
for what a face might mean when it is loved
and stares into the dark room of the world
as though that too were life, the light as kind.